OH, GROW UP!

Humanity, The Childish Species

By
Suzanne Claire

PublishAmerica
Baltimore

© 2006 by Suzanne Claire.
All rights reserved. No part of this book may be reproduced, stored in a retrieval system or transmitted in any form or by any means without the prior written permission of the publishers, except by a reviewer who may quote brief passages in a review to be printed in a newspaper, magazine or journal.

First printing

At the specific preference of the author, PublishAmerica allowed this work to remain exactly as the author intended, verbatim, without editorial input.

ISBN: 1-4241-2213-9
PUBLISHED BY PUBLISHAMERICA, LLLP
www.publishamerica.com
Baltimore

Printed in the United States of America

OH, GROW UP!

*Humanity,
The Childish Species*

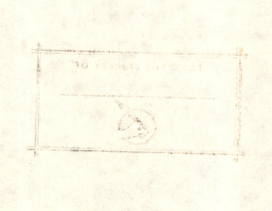

INTRODUCTION

The Platform

When the general public is asked to identify the characteristics of childhood most often the focus is on child-*like* qualities. Impressions of a positive nature are mentioned—innocent, cute, vulnerable, adorable, loveable, sweet and cuddly. Without doubt, those are real and very dear attributes that we can honestly associate with the young.

What people don't usually think of at first are the negative potentials—the things that are associated with child-*ishness*—greed, selfishness, power and control, arrogance and egotism, cruelty and violence, anger, revenge and mindless stupidity—plus—the constant need to be right all the time and in every way. Needing to be right is the active but solid foundation of all the other nasty childish attributes.

While it is true that the tendency toward those behaviors is inherent in most toddlers, it is also true that with good parenting and enlightened teaching they do not develop into the traits themselves. What is also true, however, is that without the proper care a good many of our young never do mature into responsible adults but grow up exhibiting childish responses to life from birth to death.

Today we live in a world where our species acts with an overwhelming variety of child-*ish* behavior. That there are millions of sane adults who keep trying to combat the quite horrifying results of infantile response is a given. Unfortunately, because we have let the childish control all of the major areas of our existence, the adults are in a grave and weakened minority as they try to cope with societies run by rabid bunches of Terrible Twos.

The problem is planetary. While the process may takes different paths and show different faces depending on the nation and its variations of historic and cultural development it actually doesn't take much mental effort to see that the kiddies are running things everywhere.

Childish agendas are in charge of all major elements of human activity—business and finance, politics and the military, the Media and technology, education, and, certainly, the facets of all cultural tendencies—religion, patriarchy, and sexuality. There is no single avenue down which humanity travels that is not run by the desires of the out-of-control child. As the undisciplined tot is likely to get into trouble, so is the species.

As we take our first uncertain steps into the 21st Century, it is clear that we have no coherent understanding of the dire problems facing us. We either take the attitude that science and technology will provide us with solutions to anything that might occur or we set our sights on an 'enemy' to blame for whatever is going wrong. Both excuses are not only childish, they are stupid—childish because they ignore all the current warning signs and stupid because we've had way over 10,000 years of so-called civilization to figure things out. It's one thing to be slow learners but quite another to completely ignore what's right in front of us.

As Albert Einstein said: *"Two things are infinite: The Universe and human stupidity and I'm not sure about The Universe."*

As the great scientist knew, what we call The Universe may or may not be infinite, but it's pretty certain he would now agree that the world we live in is definitely getting smaller. With the advent of instant communication and rapid travel, the planet has shrunk and is still shrinking down every day while at the same time it is showing larger and larger areas of discomfort for every living thing on it. The way things are going, it's a pretty sure bet that we will not produce any workable solutions for the self induced problems that are growing by quantum leaps every year. In fact, not only do we have no understanding that it is our childishness that causes the difficulties, we also don't see that it is the very traits of such behavior that keep us from seeing the danger.

All around the world we are neck deep in physical and verbal battles over who is right and who is wrong—the very framework seen in schoolyard fights. The virulent squabbles take place at all levels of all societies so that the arrogance that drives the child to need to be center stage at all times is now determining the fate of whole arenas of international, national and local behavior. It pits nationality against nationality, political power against political power, religion against religion and men against women. Being *right* is the excuse for childish attitudes and actions and is a force that has been allowed to drive our historical foul ups from our earliest beginnings.

Obviously, one of the main attributes of the mature adult is self-responsibility. Today we are showing more and more that we absolutely do not want to take responsibility for our choices, our decisions or our actions. Like the egotistical child who demands that The World revolve around its every whim, humanity shows very little motivation toward even the tiniest trend toward responsible behavior. We behave like the toddler who wants to be taken care of—all the time and in every way—and we most certainly do not want to take care of ourselves. What we refuse to acknowledge is that there is no one else. As the dominant species on this our planetary home, we are it! There is no great Mommy or Daddy to buy us a new toy when we break this one.

The horrific terrorist acts of September 11, 2001 and those that have followed around the globe as in Madrid, Spain; London, England and Amman, Jordan were devastating to most of the western world but were seen as not only justifiable but laudable by a large portion of the Middle East. Because neither side even wants to understand the other, the chasm between the two grows wider every day. Here the childish insistence on being right echoes around the globe. Trumpeted daily by those in power, it is the spur that kicks us into ever more forbidding situations. If it continues, and there is absolutely no sign that it won't, there will be, at some point in the not so distant future, no one left to care one way or the other. We would be wise to remember this as we look at how the power of the childish consumes every arena of our activity.

In American English the uncontrollable child is labeled a **Brat** and a bully. This tag identifies a youngster who has absolutely no concern for anything but its own desires. A Brat will go to any lengths to get what it wants and, as such, is forever totally untouched and uncaring for the pain and unhappiness of those it believes stand in its way. Hitting another kid while in the midst of a temper tantrum is natural Bratty behavior. If it makes the other child give up a toy, get off the swing or run from the room in tears, so much the better. And, if it works once, it will be repeated over and over. Today temper tantrums with lethal hitting by the Brats in power are seen in every corner of the globe. Some are nasty and violent, some are sneaky and some are even claimed to be 'legal' by those who initiate them. And because childish behavior is also all about control, the Brat will always find a way to excuse its actions. Since it stems from greed and selfishness, the desired goal is power over the situation and over other people and it is so much a part of the Brat's mindset that it is used whether or not the issue at hand is actually important or merely a trifle.

Though naturally not publicly identified as such, it was that craving for power that led those at the top of the Brat chain in America to insist on the war in Iraq. Based on holier-than-thou misrepresentations of the existence of so-called of WMDs, promotions for the war were aired with all the smugness of the toddler with a dirty diaper who blames the stench on the neighbor's dog.

We must also note that the potentials for disaster that our lack of maturity causes are now growing in accelerating blocks because of the mammoth increase in our numbers. Consider—is 1804 there were only 1 billion members of the human race on the entire planet. As of 2002 we had multiplied that to 6 billion…that's right *six billion*. In a measly 200 hundred years we over populated every livable part of the world at the same time we were busily destroying huge segments of it. As if that isn't enough on the childish stupidity scale—it is projected that by the year 2050 the number will be *nine billion*. That's another *three billion*—as in half of today's count—in just 45 little years. The majority of the 3 billion will live in poor countries and barely subsist because of the imbalance of power and control.

Every aspect and level of human activity now displays such enormous examples of childish behavior that is it impossible to open the day's newspaper or turn on the TV without finding at least a half dozen new illustrations. As we examine the major areas of modern life—corporate, political, informational, religious, medical and cultural—the Brat and its minions will be shown as the driving force behind all of them. For our survival as a species and for all other types of life that depend on us, we would be wise to be conscious of how we have let this happen.

The clock is ticking and it is way past time we looked at our need to *GROW UP!*

Chapter 1

The Money Bunnies

A Corporate World

All of the childish traits are alive and well in The Corporate World. Because this world we now live in *is* a corporate world, the tentacles of its influence have all forms of existence in a tight grip. As such, the greed and selfishness, the need for control and the mind-blowing arrogance of **The Money Bunnies** was seen in graphic detail in the summer of 2002. By that time making more money than was needed and living in a wasteful and ostentatious manner had become the sought after ideal, yet…in a split second the bloated American Dream became a gut wrenching nightmare for the country's economic stability.

Until then the highflying CEOs and Presidents of all

types of companies were envied for their wealth, their seeming skill and their swagger. They hobnobbed with political honchos and Hollywood stars. They were the reigning kings of the social elite and it was said that they were leading the country into the arms of an even more marvelous future.

Whoops...it caught nearly everyone by surprise when the corporate house of cards came tumbling down with the thundering crash of Enron, and after that fiasco hit the airwaves, it didn't take long for the public to become aware that most of the big business structure of the country was built on quick sand. Suddenly the big shots that had been the envy of all were named Stink Bugs as the depth of their fraud became known. As the number of company failures grew, so did the list of Brats who had lied, cheated and stolen to line their own pockets. The old saw about not making a silk purse out of a sow's ear was shown to be graphically true as the size of the hog wallow ballooned out across the corporate landscape.

As the scandal dragged on, some of the executives were arrested and went to trial and were actually found guilty—for example *Tyco* heads Dennis Kozlowski and Mark Swartz were each sentenced to 25 years in prison and Bernard Ebbers of *WorldCom, Inc.* got 17 to 25. Still, it would not be wise to assume that the *clean up* within the corporate scene will ever be more than a window dressing. Putting a few of the culprits in jail will not stop the rest of their buddies from finding new ways to get what they want. Just because there was quite a list of companies being investigated by the Securities and Exchange and some show boat publicity for hearings by Congress and the Labor Department during the beginning of 2004, it in no way meant a true over haul of the procedures employed to make the rich richer.

It is wise to remember that The Money Bunnies are all favored members of The Old Boys Clubs that are running the country. The childish violence that they and their kind have done to the workers, the little stockholders and the economy itself is not acknowledged as enough of a problem to make those in power change the way the system works. It could go without saying that in valued Brat fashion almost none of those charged with the scams have shown the slightest remorse or shame. They take the Fifth Amendment of silence so as not to incriminate themselves or they blatantly deny that they knew what was going on. In a weird way it can be head shaking amusing to hear the lawyers portray men who had boasted about being smarter than everyone else now pleading that they really were dumber than dirt. Moreover, the greed that led them to believe that they were entitled to buckets of ill-gotten wealth is still the major element in every corporate framework.

Whether we like it or not, money is the symbol that ignites the greed and buys the power that the childish crave and it will continue to do so unless we completely change our ways.

When an adult examines the whole idea of *money* a number of curious facts emerge. To begin with, modern money per se has no, repeat **no** intrinsic value whatsoever. Like it or not, the value of money is nothing more than a slippery and often slimy agreement to *say* it's worth something.

When the idea was first conceived 6 to 8 thousand years ago, its tokens were made of very rare metals—

gold or silver—and could, indeed, honestly be traded for goods of equal value. And because of the metals rarity only a few groups of leaders of the early cultures had coins. In every society most of the gold and silver that was found was not used for coins at all but was made into jewelry and religious and imperial icons. The people in all inhabited regions of the planet existed through barter—I give you a sack of grain, you give me a cask of beer so that I can grow more grain and you can brew more suds.

For thousands of years real wealth was in the land and it was ferociously fought for on all continents. The land was autocratically claimed by the few—kings, emperors, and religious leaders and worked by the many—peasants and slaves, but the territory, the soil itself, did have value.

Gradually, very gradually to begin with, money began to be used as an economic symbol of wealth. Different countries coined and issued their own legal tender and then fought with others over the actual value of it. After hundreds of years of squabbling, the evaluation known as the Gold Standard finally came into being in the 1870s and for a little while it assured a bit of confidence and a shaky level of equality. Once those standards were eliminated just before World War II, the whole idea of money again became a rather stinky delusion.

Today the delusion grows farther and farther away from reality. Now the remaining coinage is completely worthless and is made from cheap, abundant metals instead of gold and silver. Some coins are disguised and made to look like silver and once in a while a 'special' gold-coated commemorative piece is issued and sold as a collector's item. Otherwise, the little discs are of no real value at all when they are used around the world to make 'change' for the paper bills of the country—bills that are also worthless. Bank checks are also just fuzzy pieces of paper that promise to transfer representations of 'money' from one person or account to another.

The economically touted Credit Card creates debt not credit. And to make the slime even slicker it should be known that the person who does not owe a red cent to anyone and, therefore, has no established debt is considered by the Money Bunnies to have no credit. Anyone who is asking for a credit report but doesn't owe anything can find that out in a nano second. Aren't we cute? Never mind, its just par for the course for the Brats monetary slight of hand. After all, it is not good for the financial system if the silly consumers aren't consuming more than they can afford. Any Wall Street intern can tell you that!

Not satisfied with over 73% of American families using Credit Cards, the plastic squirrels that serve the Money Bunnies created a more honest *sounding* Debit Card. Based on money in an existing account these little beauties are directly slanted and marketed to teenage consumers. Parents are told that the Debit Cards will educate their teens in the responsible handling of money. While that might be marginally true, the real thrust of the scheme is to get the youngsters to spend more than the multi-billions they are already labeled for.

Lest we forget—whether we like it or not and no matter what the medium is called—all representations of money have no actual value; they are worth squat!

Certainly such clever manipulations of numbers makes the shifting of goods and services from one to another more convenient, but it also makes the honest and actual evaluations of those elements impossible—no matter how many corporate computations are involved. Not surprisingly, the process of setting those amounts of value is completely arbitrary and in the hands of whoever is in current control—those who wield 'economic' power.

To the hungry a loaf of bread or a pound of rice is worth life itself, to those in charge of the economic landscape, they aren't worth a proverbial, and now real, plug nickel. The power to control the value of money, or rather, what it can buy, is now the ultimate in world influence. The childish use of that power can, and does, topple nations.

It doesn't take much insight to know that the ultimate aim of the Money Bunnies, i.e. the power brokers, is to eliminate nations altogether. While that might change some of the planet's long-standing territorially based conflicts, it certainly would create many new ones. Not the least of which would be the question of what kind of power would be used to govern. Think for a moment about having world dominant corporations, bankers, accountants and stock traders as the *acknowledged* leaders of the world… That they already are the ones who control the strings of our puppet like lives is a given, if not openly stated. They create the framework of value, real or imaginary; control what we know and don't know and, of course, buy and sell politics to further their aims. That such an unbalanced power source is not taken seriously is just one more glaring proof of our total childishness.

Corporate leaders constantly evolve new systems to

enhance and strengthen their control and could care less if what occurs as a result is cruel, nasty, dangerous and monumentally stupid for the safety and well being of the planet and its inhabitants.

Consider the violence done to millions by the deliberate and carefully constructed and politically sanctioned operations around the world by the triumvirate that is made up of the International Monetary Fund, the World Bank and the U.S. Treasury.[1] Using a 4 Step plan comically titled the *Country Assistance Strategy*, this puffed up and truly sanctimonious conglomerate can send any hard up country it chooses right down the economic toilet. The process, for all countries begins with:

Step 1. *Privatization:* this is used, literally, to bribe the locals in power into selling off all of the country's assets. Once all the nation's wealth has been siphoned off its time for…

Step 2. *Capital Market Liberalization*: this is meant to sound like money can begin to flow freely both in and out of the country. What it really means is that all of its capital leaves in a rapid cascade and never comes back. It effectively *liberates* the country in question from any money it had. When those capital reserves are all gone, the IMF insists that interest rates be raised—these have been seen to go from 30% to 80% over night. Consequence…? Why, of course, it's…

Step 3. *Market Based Pricing*: this means that there will be an immediate surge in prices for the basics—food, water, domestic gas and energy, medicine and anything and everything that might make life reasonably possible for the locals.

Predictably, grinding poverty for the average citizen has been the result of the deliberate and calculated rape of the countries where the first three steps have been used. In all the nations that have been 'helped' riots have erupted...Russia, Indonesia, Ecuador, and Bolivia to name a few. Joining the unlucky group in '02 were Argentina, Uruguay and Brazil who received loans that were, as usual, guaranteed by their capital assets and subjected to the strangling conditions imposed by the IMF.

When a targeted country collapses into turmoil, the parade of impositions continues with...

Step 4. *Free Trade*: when the World Trade Organization gets into the act. If a country is granted a loan from the WTO, it comes with what are called *stipulations*. This is a buzzword that really means a set of ironclad rules designed to make absolutely sure that the flow of capital to the triumvirate is not going to be slowed or stopped, no matter what. That stream of money is the only thing that counts and it will continue to flow even if the country is falling apart at the seams. People are starving? Too bad. Dying from lack of medicine or doctors' care? So sorry. Agricultural stability devastated because there's no money to buy seed much less machinery? Ah, gee, what a pity. Schools, roads and electric power dissolving? Tut, tut.

Corporate money power and the power *of* the Money Bunnies rules, no matter what the hideous consequences of the 4 Step-plan are that sloshes childish violence over continents.

Social historians know that the last time a large portion of the planet's population focused on something besides acquiring money and amassing toys was during the Second World War. During the early 1940s the importance of sharing, of giving up not just luxuries but daily necessities was a practice embraced by men and women in most western nations. The whole idea of selfishness was abhorrent. Communities came together because it was understood by almost everyone that real world freedom was at stake. People did without and felt good about it. Certainly there was a Black Market and there were those who hoarded for their own use or for the sake of money, but neither was a big problem.

For once, even most of the corporate world cooperated and put production over profit. True, there were legal checks and balances for businesses and they had to abide by fairly stringent charter conditions or risk losing the government contracts. Even so, the main operating atmosphere surrounding most companies was one of adult responsibility.

Guns and tanks and airplanes, ships and bombs and cannons, ammunition and uniforms and parachutes were turned out by the tons as industry converted its assembly lines to supply the needs of battle. K-rations were invented and produced. *Spam* went to war! Little old ladies and school children knitted socks and afghans for the 'boys'. People who never before had grown anything more complicated than a daisy planted and harvested Victory gardens. Every thought, every plan and every asset was proudly aimed at saving the world from the horrid dictators of the Axis. Mistakes were made but, in general, the majority of the Allied population and its leaders responded to the threat as adults. The losses and the sorrows were incalculable but in the end people knew it was worth it.

Then when the war was finally over and without even a hiccup, things reverted to the old ways. Humanity immediately again began its feverish march down the road of childish consumption. The companies that had performed so well during the conflict rushed to make up in triplicate the revenue they now said they had lost. Factories were rapidly converted to peacetime products and people were hounded to buy anything and everything they could to restore prosperity. *Prosperity* became the new catchword for the promotion of greed and it was used to unite the countries that had just been bitter enemies. The nations that had been so despised — Germany, Japan and Italy — now were to be made prosperous in order to combat the rising communist threat seen coming from former friends — the Soviet Union and China. Given the nature of real economic incentive it worked beautifully for the ex-baddies on the receiving end who became bosom buddies while the old pals naturally became irate foes. The childish traits of anger, revenge, power and control, egotism, arrogance, cruelty, violence, fear and stupidity all began a tremendous upsurge in the era known as The Cold War.

Meanwhile in the U.S. new products, including the insidious TV Dinner, flooded the market. Almost all were touted as 'time savers' and 'work reducers' and were bought by the tens of millions. Along with washing machines and dryers, mixers and steam irons, nifty barbeques for the patios in the backyards of the mushrooming subdivisions and their ticky tacky little houses. Bigger and faster cars and trucks whizzed around the expanding highway systems. The continuously promoted television sets were bought for living rooms and dens all over America. It was said to be patriotic to buy the country into prosperity and everyone wanted to play. When an over abundance of toys is said to be the foundation of The Good Life, childish greed is embraced by all.

And so, as our story goes, the nation basked for nearly two decades in self-satisfaction while it consumed at an unheard of rate. The greed that was on such a stupendous rise was still masked somewhat by the terrible events of the 40s as well as the still remembered poverty and despair of the Great Depression of the 30s. There was a short backlash during the 60s and early 70s over the horror and stupidity of the Vietnam War, but it didn't take long for the Hippie movement that raised the issue of over consumption along with disgust for the war in 'Nam' to be effectively squashed by those who had gotten a taste of lip licking consumerism. Aided by a government that could not stand by while a growing segment of the population toyed with the idea of anarchy, corporate America simply out spent, out squawked and out maneuvered Flower Power. The Hipsters didn't believe in *making* anyone do anything anyway and so did not organize enough to combat those who wanted to convert them.

History shows that in the end the ex-Hippie contributed in a big way to the rising number of people who eventually jumped on the Yuppie- *Me First* train that roared through the 70s and 80s. That train sped toward such levels of greed and selfishness that the corporate hierarchy was giggling in disbelief. It was thought for a while that the *Me Generation* had shown the world the highest form of gluttony since the late

Roman Empire and that it could not be topped—that was, however, before the dawn of the 90s.

The fantastic 90s saw the sudden rise and mutation of the new technological companies whose 'earnings' put the greed and arrogance of the earlier decade to shame. It didn't matter that much of the wealth was built on hot air and fancy accounting footwork, everyone wanted a part of it and bought in by the millions. Wall Street squeaked with delight and pumped shares for profit from the Opening Bell to its closing. Millionaires were no longer the rich, there were too many of them. In the 90s the *rich* were billionaires who, by and large, still didn't think they had enough. Tekkie hot shots lied, bribed and stole to get a jump on competitors and often bragged about it.

Media stories during that decade displayed greed proudly in showcases like Silicon Valley and reported it as the norm for the new rich. The public simply groaned in envy when teased with pictures of houses as big as hotels and enough luxury cars to start a limo service. Naturally, none of the owners was ever described as greedy; they were said to be smart. Their childish egotism and arrogance was seen as setting the tone for *stylish* behavior.

In the larger scheme of things, the Media celebration of such individuals would not matter one way or the other if, as a group, they were not setting the standards for the whole culture. With their wealth so graphically displayed and touted, it made everyone eager to be like them. 13 year olds couldn't wait to invent some technological gizmo in order to become over night millionaires. Enough of them had done it to make the idea something a kid believed could happen. And...since the atmosphere of the times indulged young and old with enough toys to have Santa hopping 365 days a year, there was nothing to keep the lust from growing.

The downturn of the economy after the tragedy of 9/11, did not repeat, did not, change the nation's inclination toward avarice. It simply clothed it in patriotism. Less than a year after the attacks the population again heard the ancient cry of the need to buy the country back into…uh huh…*Prosperity*! Politicians used the old slogan again and again while they sent the country plunging from a healthy government surplus into a glowering deficit. Corporations followed suit while the Stock Market tanked and once hallowed companies fought bankruptcy and lawsuits.

The gadget business that had fueled the money rush of technology was the hardest hit in the months following 9-11. In an effort to stave off complete collapse, the old scheme called Designed Obsolescence that had been used in the gluttonous years of the 90s was pushed into high gear. Using this creepy process, manufacturers simply create 'new' forms of old toys that won't work in conjunction with their earlier ones. By changing products so that the *improved* versions are incompatible with the previous ones, the consumer has to buy whole new systems in order to do exactly what he was doing in the first place.

Gimmicks and frippery are advertised as allowing the user to *up grade* and to *keep up with the latest technology* while the real reason behind creating them is nothing more than a ploy to boost sales. With the skill and efficiency that's available it would be quite simple for the producers to make the 'improvements' work with the older versions but such an adult choice would never be allowed by a Money Bunny; it wouldn't bring in the cabbage. Sometimes the new toy doesn't even work as well as the displaced one. As they say Down Under, "no worries". The flop ears could care less that what they are selling is basically dishonest and contrived; anything is fair if it fills their pockets.

For example...in August of '02 Jane Spencer of The Wall Street Journal documented that shorter warranties and design changes meant '...that buyers of even relatively expensive gadgets now have little choice but to throw them in the trash if anything breaks."[2] The proof behind her complaint is the fact that a lot of manufacturers now build their little cuties in one piece sealed units. This means that even if parts were available, which they are not, it would be impossible to get inside the units. Yes, some products are just glued shut, but the heat needed to get them open is so high it would effectively damage the piece as a whole. Needless to say, companies are doing a lot less product testing, why bother...if it's good for business when something breaks, let's let 'em break sooner and more often. Never mind that it puts another horrid strain on the already over flowing landfills and garbage dumps, caring for the environment is not something the Brats consider important.

A natural result of the break 'n' throw process is that customer service is now worse than ever—after all, it's not particularly good marketing to tell customers that you deliberately built the gadget badly so they would have to buy a new one. Do the Board members and stockholders of the companies care that the products that they have an interest in are deliberately being built to fail? Hardly! The Cash Cow is sacred and it takes constant feeding. If producing shoddy merchandise keeps the money rolling in, it becomes the darling method of choice. At all levels the egotism of the Brat is quite comfortable with the idea that caring for the customer is bad for business.

In an adult world the buyers would stop buying the products, would set up a storm of protest and might even take the failed products and dump them outside company headquarters—by the ton. In case it hasn't been noticed yet, we do not live in an adult world.

The irony of it is that it is the so-called *adult* toys that drive a lot of the technocratic greed, so it is not surprising that they are the fizzy gimmicks that have invaded the office, the home, the college campus, the automobile and grown up play grounds.[3] There is no arena in today's society that has not been flooded with them. The cell phone rings, we jump, Never mind that we are driving a car, making our way through a crosswalk, at a baseball game or at the super market. The makers of the beeping pests would be delighted to have them installed in coffins, if they could just convince people it was a great way to communicate with the dear departed.

Manufacturers want their gimmicks used in every possible situation and so do the large corporations that now buy them in vast quantities. The companies know that the more tightly they can make their employees stay connected to the *office*, the more tightly they can control them. While honor, integrity and honesty are flapped around as the main objectives of the work environment, today Bratty control is the essential name of the game.

Take vacation time...it used to be that this was an acknowledged and much needed opportunity to get away from the daily grind for a little while. It was a small chance to establish a sense of balance and to nourish a worn out mind and body, which, in turn, would make a worker more productive. Now there is no such time allowed to the working slob connected to the toys. There have even been ads on TV showing the office grunt on a beach busily punching away at his traveling fidgets. The sales come-on is that you don't have to give up your *important* duties in order to spend time on the beach. What's studiously not mentioned is that if you're working you might as well not *be* at the beach. If you're reading office memos, answering dozens of emails or rewriting a report that the boss dreamed up yesterday, no relaxation is involved. In the corporate world a worker's value is determined by how much work can be squeezed out for as little money as possible.

This reality was underlined early in the year 2004 when the flap about the business procedure known as Out Sourcing was made public. Information about the process began hitting the airwaves in February and identified that hundreds of companies of all kinds of businesses were hiring workers in other countries in order to pay much lower wages and to give fewer or no benefits. While much of this was being done in the arena of technology, the practice literally covered the corporate map in its variety of goods and services. It was thought to be a brilliant concept by management honchos and their financial advisors even as offices and factories were being abandoned all across the country and more and more people were added to the already large numbers of those out of work.

Even the numbers that supposedly tallied how many local workers were displaced were shown to be wrong because so many people had given up looking for jobs. The percentage touted by those who wanted to say that the economy wasn't so bad was 5.6% whereas the real number was 7.4%...a sweet little sample of childish arrogance wedded with a lie.

For once, the Media onslaught over Out Sourcing was loud and bitter. The corporations doing it couldn't have cared less; the Bottom Line was all that mattered. They did a little public relations blabber about how it would, in the long run, be good for the economy since it would, according to them, open up new areas of investment, but the arguments were pretty lame and certainly didn't convince those hurt by the process.

Interestingly, for once many of the economic pundits were outraged. One was Lou Dobbs, the respected host of the CNN financial program, The Lou Dobbs Money Hour. This man, long known for his by-the-book market place theories was so appalled he made public a daily list of the companies that were engaging in Out Sourcing. He went so far as to get into on-air arguments with those who tried to defend the practice. He expressed his disgust, but there were few signs that any of this money mongering behavior would stop or decline any time soon, if ever. When a company can pay a dollar or a dollar and a quarter in India for an hours work that used to cost it twelve or twenty dollars here at home, it doesn't care what is being said or by whom.

While corporations and many smaller companies insisted that their employees carry a cell phone or a gadget size computer before Out Sourcing became a business as usual choice, the practice has now become almost universal. The company 'gives' the doo-hickey to the worker and pays a bulk rate service charge not available to individual users. In exchange it demands that a response can be requested at any time, day or night. If the employee doesn't like it, he or she can bloody well lump it or be replaced in a nanosecond. After all, there are plenty of people who are hurting and will take any kind of job just to try to get by and since the once powerful unions have little clout in today's business structure they really can't be counted on to do anything to help.

Amazingly, to an adult, there are scads of people who actually brag about the fact that they are constantly glued to what's satirically called a 'hand held digital assistant'. One corporate Vice President who was getting 200 to 300 emails a day was publicly puffed up about the fact that he could reply no matter where he was or who it was. Yes, Virginia, he's the idiot at the next table in the restaurant talking on his cell phone, punching away at his itty-bitty keyboard and glugging martinis. In some places this kind of Bratty behavior has gotten so bad that signs are being posted that prohibit the use of these toys in a large variety of establishments.

The raft of goodies produced after World War II were continuously and loudly hyped as being time and effort savers and great erasers of the burdens of existence. The ploy worked then and it works now, even if the opposite is true about 99% of the time. Granted, the first clothes dryers did make doing the laundry easier and did save time and were particularly appreciated during the middle of a winter snowstorm. What we tend to forget, however, is that the real aids to physical well being were invented and produced quite a while ago and are uniformly taken for granted by most Americans.

In-door plumbing, illumination, heating and cooling are so much a part of the modern landscape that most people rarely notice them unless the power goes out or there is a break in the water main. Likewise stoves, refrigerators, freezers and microwave ovens are in practically every home so that cooking and storing food is a cinch. The food itself is in abundance in huge supermarkets or people can buy the constantly advertised Fast Food that makes even walking into the kitchen unnecessary. The fact that the FF doesn't require any taste buds and has been a major player in national obesity doesn't matter—it makes a lot of big bucks for a raft of worldwide chains.

Even in a depressed economy food, water and shelter, three actual necessities of life, are so available to such a large majority of Americans that it's the considered opinion of the business world that they really don't matter anymore. More than ever, its focus is now on the 'goodies'.

Since the only criteria of worth in a capitalistic society is whether or not something will sell, all kinds of commercial oddities abound. In other words, if something will bring in the moola, it doesn't matter a whit if it's silly, stupid, useless, ugly, mind numbing or even potentially dangerous. The more a product caters to public greed, the better. Two examples from very different ends of the value spectrum serve to illustrate how corporate ego and avarice benefit from those same childish traits in the customer.

The first is what was to become known as The Beanie

Baby Craze. Small stuffed animal dolls filled with—um...*beans*—became such a cash cow for the maker that every company on the planet was envious. It's no secret that historically dolls have been a part of the human experience almost from our beginnings. They've been made of every possible material on every continent. The doll has given comfort, been a friend and helped soothe kiddy fears and nightmares. It has been used as a religious representation, a focus in literature and, gradually, has become a favorite advertising tool. The Beanies were different—they only advertised themselves. Moreover, they weren't meant to be played with, they were simply to be collected. That is to say, they were to be *bought*.

The marketing ploy was ingenious and worked like a charm right from the beginning. A tiny stuffed animal would be released for a limited time and then abruptly taken off the market. If the collector missed getting that one, the collection couldn't be complete—unless—and here's where the childish greed and control took over—it could be bought off another collector. The competition got so fierce that people were lining up at two, three, and four in the morning outside toy stores where local police often had to be called in to preserve the peace.

Stores had to limit the number of a new release that could be purchased by one individual since the earliest customers would try to buy up the entire stock. They knew that by holding onto that edition they could ask an outlandish price for it once it was retired from manufacture. Even with the rule the merchants were running out of beans in a very short time—while late arriving buyers complained bitterly to the local and national reporters covering the story. The manufacturer was ecstatic at the free media coverage and the enormous sales, the outlet stores were delighted and mothers and fathers got into physical fights trying to grab the dolls.

As time went on parents showing off their 'children's' collections on TV became a wonderfully glaring example of Brat behavior. Whole walls filled with shelves of the Beanies were exhibited for the cameras. Often a small child would hover on the sidelines, not quite sure what was going on since it was obvious they were not allowed to play with the toys. Not surprisingly, older children caught on quickly and learned to brag about how they had more Beanies than their friends. The feeding frenzy went on for several years and while similar products hit the market, none could ever compete with the corporate success of the original.

While the example of the legume filled dolls proved that people could be very easily manipulated to show their childish tendencies and be proud of them, it was still just a one-time blip on the social scene. Though it brought the maker millions in profit and pumped the Brat ego of the collectors, it was just another example of the direction that U.S. consumerism had been stumbling down for a long time. As such, it wasn't given much sociological or psychological attention.

Our second example is more telling and concerns the deliberate marketing of extreme violence to children. A report by the Federal Trade Commission for the year 2000 graphically accused the entertainment industry of targeting youngsters under the age of 17 with overt advertising practices for the sale of violent films, recordings and video games. While corporate greed was the usual prime motivation, it was the childish arrogance of the perpetuators that made them sure they could get away with it. The FTC's accusation made note of the fact that the companies involved knew all along that the products they were touting weren't just inappropriate but basically against all sorts of trade laws. The flap of outrage that arose was big enough to cause Congressional hearings and massive Media coverage and as expected set off a storm of pious speeches and pompous posturing. Did it stop the process? Nah…Five years later it was still ridiculously easy for the kids to find and purchase all kinds of products extolling violence. As ever, the producers simply backtracked, looked around and found new ways to promote their nasty wares. When the Money Bunnies are raking in the carrots by the bushels, violence isn't just OK, it's sweet and juicy. Besides, they know that the kiddies are being conditioned to violence from the first moment they plop down in front of a TV set. Check out the cartoon channels for the best in bang, bang shoot-em ups and wipe-em outs. Sure the 'good' guys always win, but that doesn't excuse the brainwashing of the tots to believe that violence is fun. Certainly cartoons have always relied on violence for plot enhancement but the old characters were pure fantasy and did not portray many children as the perpetrators. Wile E. Coyote and Road Runner, Tom and Jerry or Bugs and Elmer went through horribly nasty fights but they were so far from reality that kids instinctively knew it wasn't real. Today the most popular series show kids as both the good guys and the bad guys and the battles are lethal. The step from cartoons to movies is a short one. In November of 2005 it was reported by Sandy Cohen that the level of violence in 'children's' cinema was increasing rapidly. [4] Such negative statements don't bother the corporations one little bit—violence and smut are lucrative.

In everyday terms, the childishness seen in the corporate world is simply part of the game. What's not understood and rarely even mentioned, is that all of the traits of that childishness are built in components of Capitalism and have been from its beginning. As a matter of standard procedure, each company wants all of its potential market—no ifs, ands or buts about it. The much-trumpeted idea of *competition* that is supposed to provide opportunity for all is actually so much blather. Every kind of business is utterly devoted to making sure it has as little competition as possible and would prefer it if there was none at all. Mergers, take-overs, buy-outs, sleazy advertising and the under cutting of competitors prices are common methods of economic greed and the desire for total control...as are collusion, lying and stealing. As seen in the rash of corporate scandals, the bigger the business, the more ruthless its attacks on the competition. The loudest trumpet blared by those trying to hog the market is the old line that it's of benefit to the consumer to have lots of choices all the while making damn sure that the poor consumer doesn't have any choice at all. The suppliers of all types of goods have become so huge, cover so many kinds of products and have no qualms about advertising against themselves that the buyers' dollars generally wind up in just a few big accounts.

A prime example that affects the entire population is seen in the grocery business. A study shows thousands of different brand names all belong to the same producers.

The 'smart' shopper may try to compare brands for the best product...not an easy task. The print on the labels is either so tiny it can't be read without a magnifying glass or is stated in gibberish. If the buyer tries to get information from a Consumer Reference phone number he winds up stuck with the 'press 1 for our blah blah, press 2 for a ga ga, press 3 for la la...' When the recording has gone through ten or more 'instructions' it simply reverts to press one for...By that time the shopper needs a cool drink of water and a quiet nap. Mega corporations do everything they can to keep the prospective purchaser in the dark about how they really operate since to them, fabricated competition works best.

For example...the average shopper certainly was not aware that as of the year 2000 there were just five—right, **five**—major world corporations marketing food and grocery outlet household items like toilet paper and soap.[5] Ever heard of Nestle S A, Phillip Morris-Nabisco, Unilever-Bestfoods, ConAgr, Inc. and, of course, Pillsbury-General Foods? The mergers and takeovers that created these mega-monsters show right in the double names and simply underline the obvious...when such a death grip is held on the most purchased brands of grocery store products there is not the slightest hint of competition. Prices can go up and down across the board while deliberate but violent swings in costs can be blamed on 'economic conditions' whenever the participants choose. They know that since food and home care products are necessities they will be bought no matter what. Evidence of back door arrangements is apparant when so-called competitors alternate with 'special' price cuts every other week. Gorillas like Coca

Cola and Pepsi can just take turns lowering the cost of a carton of their drinks every other week. Never fear...they've been able to up the prices enough over the last few years that they still make incredible profits.

It doesn't take a Masters Degree in Economics to understand that the mergers going on at the beginning of the 21st Century are nothing more than a deliberate effort at an expansion of the markets to be held by an even smaller number of companies. That the process is continuously pumped as being a method to improve service and offer better prices is another self-serving lie; everyone loses but the perpetrators. The Brat will say anything that helps it get its own way...so sometimes the mergers are called *consolidations* and are advertised as making companies leaner and more efficient. Leaner? Yes! Half the hired hands in overlapping departments are fired and those that are kept are expected to do the work of two people. More efficient? Yes, if you define that as fewer hands doing more work over longer hours for no increase in pay. This type of childish cruelty is now a business standard.

That's not to say that we've come up with an adult way to produce and market goods. Communism proved how selfish kiddies will always make sure that they rise to the top with crass displays of theft and corruption. The bullies of the Kremlin were able to stash huge fortunes in Swiss banks and built luxury dachas while the Russian people starved. The resulting mess took such a toll and decades later a lot of the country is still in the tight grasp of poverty. Pure Socialism didn't fare much better and has mostly faded from the world scene. What we don't understand or even study is that it is not the process that leads our species into such catastrophic idiocy; it is the Brats running it and the lackeys they attract through the childish manipulation of greed.

Under Capitalism the manipulation of greed has led to an abundance of examples that show how far we are from a standard of adult behavior. The huge Bridgestone/Firestone Tire and Ford Motor Company fiasco finally became public in the summer of 2000 is a graphic illustration.[6] It was known by Firestone that certain of its tires were causing accidents and death *eight* whole years before the story broke in the United States. The problems with tread separation first came to corporate notice in 1992 but were deliberately kept secret. Why? Well gee...most of the early accidents, injuries and deaths caused by the faulty tires had occurred in other countries and Firestone didn't want to *alarm* its U.S. buyers market. Ford was to become linked to the disasters because they used the Firestone tires and the cars were not stable so they rolled over a lot.

For eight years the companies hopped merrily down the Bunny Trail but finally after ninety deaths and hundreds of injuries in America, the truth could not be kept hidden.

At the beginning of the scandal in America 6.5 million tires were placed on the deficient list that was authorized for recall and many more were to follow. The story ignited the usual hearings in Congress and the Senate and sparked both individual and class action law suits against Firestone and Ford.

During this period, executives from both companies went public with TV ads apologizing for the predicament at the same time their businesses were furiously backpedaling to keep from being held at fault. Saying,

"I'm sorry," became the chosen method to try and shift focus and the VIPs had no shame in using it. Like the Brat who says it's sorry and doesn't mean it, it was simply meant to shift blame.

As the hearings on the cover ups about the bad tires plodded on, it became pretty clear that Firestone and Ford would do anything necessary to delay any final decisions on liability. The childish arrogance of their stalling went on for months and months as each tried to blame the other for the accidents. Firestone denied responsibility by saying that their adversary's cars and trucks were prone to the rollovers while Ford insisted it was the fault of the tire treads slippage. In the end, both were found to be right because both were found to be wrong—the vehicles did roll and the tires were bad.

As stated, the whole reason for not stepping up to the plate and admitting and addressing the problems at the outset was the threat to the market status of both companies. The so-called good name of the Firestone and Ford brands translated into billions of dollars. Selling dangerous products was not the issue; increasing profits was. How many people knew what was going on from the beginning will probably never be revealed to the public, and not one of those individuals involved had enough honesty or courage to buck the threat of retribution from the corporate jackals in charge. What's shown in this example is that Brat policy and procedure had been corrupting the business world long before the explosion of Enron.

It also identifies the type of childish cruelty and violence that accompanies such callous decisions. As such it was carried out in two distinct forms—overt and hidden. Overt brutality crowds the pages of the daily newspapers and clogs the television screen continuously but the under the table type is so much a product of corporate collusion that it takes a debacle the size of the Firestone/Ford scandal to bring it out in the open. The accidents and deaths were certainly violent in themselves, but it was the deliberate and calculated decision to keep them quiet for eight years that displayed the worst kind of deadly, childish behavior. No amount of apology or money can make up for deliberately made choices that put people in danger of death and injury.

Given the combined addiction for control and eternally increased revenue that drives all corporations, it's not surprising that the egotism that is an international business standard allows unethical practices to thrive. The chant heard around the globe that a company exists for the good of the customer is a lovely little excuse for the power freaks at the top to do exactly as they please which is why they were stunned when the corporate meltdowns of '02 came rushing down the economic pike. That the deadly cancers had been building for over a decade was obvious. That those in charge were complacent in their arrogance and confident in their positions of power was what allowed the fraud to happen in the first place. The last thing a Brat ever expects is that it will be thwarted in any of its actions, no matter how awful.

When one Brat group sees another of its kind getting the goodies, the scramble to get more becomes vicious. The telecommunications conglomerates lead the pack in looking for ways to soak the user for more money. For years the long distance phone companies spent mega millions on advertising to promote the idea that their rates were lower than any of their competitors. Since all of them were doing it, we can be certain that most, if not all, were lying.

Cell phone users have to cope with the hocus pocus offered by their providers. When the telecom stock values sank a hefty 70% in 2002 the companies went straight to the customers to bail them out of the financial meltdown that the companies themselves had created. In August 2002, Reid J. Epstein of The Wall Street Journal reported that all the wireless providers were upping their charges. He noted that at Sprint PCS it was decided to deduct from all monthly allotment plans time that their customers would spend to check on *how many minutes they had left* on those same plans. The company also added a $3.00 charge for each and every call to a 'Customer Service' Rep.

At the same time Epstein reported that Cingular Wireless chose to charge 10 cents for each text message received—whether it was ever read or not, while Nextel changed its policy to round up all fractions of minutes to the next full minute. Before, 1 minute and 02 seconds would have added up to 1 minute and 10 seconds, the new charge would be for 2 full minutes. By tacking on pennies and charging for services that had been free, a whopping 2 to 3 percent of total revenue would be realized. Throughout the telecom industry, that kind of increase works out to about 2 billion dollars a year. Companies can pay measly fines in the millions when they are sued and still chortle all the way to the bank. From month to month and year to year the schemes change constantly with 'new' offers and highly advertised 'discounts' but like it or not, the dizzy consumer will continue to be played for a fool.

In spite of all the hoo hah generated by the scandals of '02, little was ever said about the Telecommunications Deregulations Act of 1996 though it had been a direct cause of the problems. One of the few people who did focus on it was Bob McChesney, media critic and professor at Southern Illinois University who pointed a very critical finger at what had really been behind the blowup. Professor McChesney wrote: "The Telecommunications Act of 1996 was one of the most important of the last 50 years. It was also one of the most corrupt and undemocratic bills of the time. It was of, by and for special interests. Most of the congressional reps who voted for it didn't even know what they were voting on."

What he was referring to was the fact that in 1996 there were 12 big phone companies—as of 2002 the number was down to 6. As of 2005 more mergers and takeovers were still being fought over in order to decrease the number even further. The 1996 legislation had made possible the childish shenanigans of Global Crossing and WorldCom that were right at the top of the scandal list but no one was talking about it. So when WorldCom went pfft, rival corporate vultures were already circling. In 2005 Verizon swooped down and hauled off WC's stinky carcass after a claw and talon fight with Quest Communications.

Another huge example that rams home the reality that the corporate world lacks any shame or regret for its childish actions goes back to 1990 and the Exxon Valdez oil spill in Prince William Sound, Alaska. The 11 million gallon spill affected 1,200 miles of coastline, destroyed a flourishing fishing business that was the sole support for not only families but towns and villages, killed at least 36,000 migratory birds, over a thousand sea otters, unaccountable salmon and herring and decimated beaches that a decade and a half later still gurgle with oil pockets in the sand.

Since 1990, fishermen and natives as plaintiffs and Exxon as defendant have battled in the courts. In 1991 the State of Alaska, the U.S. Justice Department and Exxon arranged a deal that would allow the oil giant to plead guilty to four *misdemeanor* environmental charges where it would put up $100 million for criminal penalties and $900 million for civil damages. And...as long as the world's eyes and ears were tuned to the story, Exxon made like Goody Two Shoes about the clean up and compensation. Once the Media coverage died down, the company reverted to the usual corporate response to its mistakes and began a barrage of counter attacks and procedural delays. Finally, in May of 1994 a trial began in the Federal Courthouse in Anchorage. On September 16, a federal jury came in with an order for Exxon to pay $5.2 billion in punitive damages to the civilian defendants. True to form and almost before the jury Foreman had stopped speaking, the company filed over two dozen post-trial motions. Still, it only took a mere year to close those out.

The case was trotted over to the Ninth Circuit Court of Appeals in 1998 and primly squatted there until November of 2001 when the $5.2 billion dollar award was overturned as being 'excessive'. Sent back to the District Court, it wasn't until January 2004 that a new amount was announced: $4.3 billion. Not too bad...Exxon had earned $2 billion dollars in interest on money the company had invested in 1994 to cover the award. Never mind that in the 15 years since the spill about 1000 of the original claimants had died without one cent of compensation. Naturally, Exxon immediately had appeals ready to post in court so it could effectively stall that latest verdict.

Environmental disasters occur through man's idiocy or through the mighty forces of nature as shown by the end of summer hurricanes Katrina and Rita that swept through the gulf coast in 2005. In both cases the Money Bunnies find ways to make and keep money that by all rights should not belong to them. The mismanagement of the response to the storm has been well documented but when we're talking about the corporate and political Brats who showed how little they really cared, there is one arena that deserves a bit of late notice...the reconstruction platform. On back pages of newspapers there were a few little stories that talked about the non bid contracts that were being awarded to the companies that lined the politicians' pockets and then nestled warmly in them. Not only did the favored corporations not have to bid to get the jobs they also were, by government decree, allowed to under pay their workers. Meaning? They could charge the government a high price for the projects while getting extra doubloons by cutting the hourly wage to a below market price...some were even smaller than the minimum wage. In other words, a number of rich corporations were going to get richer by sticking it to the poor who had already been beaten to a bloody pulp by the hurricanes. One guess at which corporation led the list? Uh-huh...Halliburton. Way to go Dickey!

Finally, a few words about the path the so-called economy has taken under the leadership of Federal Reserve Chairman, Alan Greenspan.[7] He will be remembered fondly by those who delight in seeing the government stripped of any need to provide for the sick, the old or the poor. That he has always been what's known as a political hack will quietly be kept out of the plaudits. That he has helped change the entire economic landscape to one of gut wrenching ideology is a given. At the same time he was making sure the Bunnies had control of the market while the 'real' basis of financial stability—the combination of work and production—was kicked out of town. He has endorsed all of the Money Bunnies 'plans' put forth to 'stabilize' the economy—all of which have done just the opposite. By late in '05 many jittery financial advisors were beginning to see the real possibility of a depression but most were afraid to talk very much about it since the overt possibility of fear could help hasten its arrival.

As stated at the beginning...we live in a corporate world that now has its eyes set on having control of every kind of human activity. It makes inroads every day and already resembles a fanged monster that takes delight in eating everything and everyone in sight. Examples of its childishness are found in the business section of each and every day's paper. The sleaze that erupts around major stories makes for excited reporting for a day or two and then dies down and is forgotten. Even when one of the Brats is found guilty and sent to jail, it's just a blip on the Media screen and has no real impact on the system.

While the American public may think itself a bit wiser and warier from knowing about the 2002 scandals, it also ought to know by now that its concerns do not really matter. The Money Bunnies may shift things around to look good but they will actually change nothing of importance. As long as they are allowed to control how and where goods and services are produced, priced and delivered—the consumer will continue to pay through the nose for stuff that may or may not be worth having in the first place. And as long as they have the politicians in debt for huge donations, they will indeed stay in control.

CHAPTER 2
The Polliwogs

Government and Politics

At the beginning of the 21st Century the world of government and politics in America had all the qualities of a chapter out of *Alice In Wonderland*. It would be easy to pin the labels of Cheshire Cat, Mad Hatter, and The Queen of Hearts on any number of the most important individuals in Washington and around the country. That story about a loony trip down a rabbit hole is, after all, a children's book and what went on in the political landscape in '04 was every bit as childish and just as nuts. Dissecting the fractured state of the political stage would be highly amusing, if it was not so dangerous and had not been becoming more so for a painfully long time. For example, as the first year anniversary of the 9/11 attacks approached at the beginning of September, the gap between the real and the illusionary became profound.

It started when Congress, in a loud statement of 'solidarity' made a symbolic trip to New York to hold a special session in Federal Hall where the members sang and posed for the cameras in front of the dear old flag. No doubt about it, people all over the country got lumps in their throats and tears in their eyes watching the theatrical spectacle. Spectacles are designed specifically by political planners to pump up every possible reaction on the plus side and to tamp down or nullify any negative response. When the red, white and blue of the nation's inclination to patriotism can be tapped, every elephant and donkey lines up for the photo ops. Of course the congressional tadpoles felt sympathy and sorrow, but the event itself was a kiddie display of egotism and power.

This was going on while the signals were getting stronger every day that the economy had not yet hit bottom as thousands of people were losing jobs, the list of company bankruptcies continued to grow and all kinds of stocks continued to sink in value. Medical costs zoomed upward as HMO rates climbed 20%, Social Security money was being used for unrelated government payouts and the school systems were in trouble from pre-kindergarten through college. People were appalled but not particularly surprised when word leaked out that almost a majority of college students tested out with way, way below average reading skills. The No Child Left Behind schmooze was working…it was making sure that *every* child was left behind so that the framework that provided public education for the peasants would eventually collapse.

What were **The Polliwogs** in charge of government doing about these basic problems to national stability? Practically speaking, nothing!

Two subjects were all the politicians focused on: a potential war in Iraq and upcoming mid-term elections. President Bush managed to concentrate on both as he flew non-stop around the land raising money for Republican candidates and trumpeting the need to remove Saddam Hussein. Administration spokesmen declined to answer questions concerning the whys and wherefores of the sudden escalation of the battle cries on the ground that it would be dangerous to the safety of the country to do so. They also had the Brat's nerve to insist that secrecy in all, repeat all, of their actions was warranted in local, national and international arenas.

The GOP Polliwogs knew that hammering the ears of the public with the drums of war was a sure way to keep some of its focus off the dustbin of economic news. Keeping the economy in the background, if not wholly under the rug, was imperative to the party's fanatic march toward keeping their majority in the House and in defeating the Democrats hold on the Senate—both of which were teetering against them in the wake of the corporate scandals and almost total lack of effort focused on the country's needs.

The childish urgency for the complete control of political power was both overt and deliberate but it took a lot of searching through the Media outlets to find any adult analysis of the constant use of scare tactics being used to divert people's attention. The arrogance of possibly sending thousands to probable death or injury was barely mentioned while the stupidity of ignoring a disaster in the aftermath of a unilateral invasion of Iraq was not raised as an issue. The arrogance of the Administration was palpable—they 'knew better' than anyone else and were not slow to say so.

The duplicity of the parade of militarism by the government is mind blowing to a grown up.[1] In August it can say that Hussein is to be attacked because he might have nuclear weapons, while in March of the same year it had been pushing for the creation of a program that would design, build and be able to deploy baby nukes...little bitty bombs that could be carried in a suitcase but wipe out whole countryside. In other words, if Saddam has it, it's bad; if we have it, it's good. Pentagon officials said publicly that they were studying the need to develop 'theater' nukes designed for use against specific targets on a battlefield. One report went so far as to say that the Pentagon should be prepared to use nuclear weapons in the Arab-Israeli conflict, in a war between China and Taiwan, in an attack from North Korea to South Korea, and, of course, against Iraq. The childish "I'm right, you're wrong," was all the proof of need that anyone ever heard.

The politics of war can be used to divide a country, to unite a country or to deceive a country and they can all be used at the same time.

When the Founding Fathers developed the principles and laws designed to implement the then new concept of a democratic state, they were rebelling against the conditions forced on a population by monarchies. Generally speaking, their aims were pure, their ideals lofty and their dedication sincere. Granted, there were elements within the culture that were despicable—

slavery was an accepted practice and women were considered incapable of serious thought much less real intelligence. Also, only those who owned land were given the right to vote. Still, the intent was better than anything conceived in earlier ages and those in charge mainly conducted themselves as adults who believed in honesty, integrity and ethical behavior.

The colonies for which they drew up the Articles of Confederation were thinly populated and were confined to small tracts of land along the eastern seaboard. News was slow to reach the citizens but was seriously debated by them personally when they did hear what was going on. The public's opinion was part and parcel of its government and could not be ignored by any of those voted into office.

Today just the opposite is true.

Not only do the politicians do their best to ignore public opinion, they go out of their way to make sure people have no idea what's really going on. Politics is marketed like Fast Food and often is just as hard to swallow and as bad or worse for the health and well being of the consumer. The word used to describe the process of slanting or altering the meaning of a candidate's stand on an issue is called *spin* and it truly can leave the listener reeling.

From 2000 to the beginning of 2004, honesty was the last thing that those promoting a political opinion wanted to have heard. Selling the client to the voter was the only thing that mattered. If a candidate was in cahoots with corporate polluters, he was spun as an environmentalist. If he played footsie with the medical insurance and prescription drug companies, he was said to be worried about Medicare and Medicaid. If he was a straight conservative against women's rights and the separation of church and state, he was passed off as a staunch supporter of better education and that old garbage dumpster *Family Values*. It didn't matter what or who a candidate really was—the voter was not supposed to know anyway. The Brat never, ever has any shame about lying to get what it wants.

The other technique used to hype the political process in 2000 and the midterms in 2002 was the virulent onslaught of nasty negative advertising. A smear campaign started by one side was immediately answered by the other. While the GOP was much better at it than the DEMs, the results made a schoolyard brawl look down right friendly. Not only did the candidates and their handlers show themselves willing to say anything in order to win, they also adeptly avoided taking a stand on real issues by that constant slinging of mud.

The whole procedure was obviously childish but had become so much a part of The Polliwog landscape it was taken for granted—and the more it was ignored, the worse it became. Give a Brat an inch and it will take the proverbial mile. When political power and control are involved it becomes miles and miles…and miles…

Behind every political battle for power we find the manipulation of money. In the Presidential race of 2000 it became so outlandish that the number of dollars being raised was posted almost daily by the media. Citizens were disgusted. Citizens were outraged. Citizens were helpless to do anything about it.

Senator John McCain, R-AZ, made the issue part of his platform as a contender for Republican Candidate for

President. He had good strong backing, was a refreshingly believable, honest speaker and a decorated Vietnam veteran. He scared George W. Bush's camp mightily. So—their time-tested responses were to smear him continuously and to ask for, and get, more money from their corporate sponsors.

Meanwhile both parties bandied around the idea of campaign finance reform like soggy shuttlecocks. Everyone knew it was pretty meaningless. After all, if you allow reform, you don't get the money and if you don't get the money, you might not get re-elected, so you can't continue to wield your power to convince the vote. Convincing the vote is crucial since it is the way to your continuing power and of course, more money.

Later when McCain and Democratic Senator Russ Feingold sponsored a reform bill it took two years to get out of Senate Committee.[2] By then, it had been so watered down it wouldn't make much difference anyway. And since it wouldn't become the law until the midterms in '02, it allowed a nice little loophole for piling up the bucks. By scrabbling for donations they would have a hefty bankroll left over for the Presidential fight of '04. By late 2003 the Bush war chest had amassed nearly $200,000,000—two hundred million—and was still stumping for more.

If a political party has spent millions to corral the vote and still isn't sure of the outcome, all sorts of Polly Woggle Doodles come into play. No example comes close to challenging the fun and games that were seen in the State of Florida by a world audience at the end of the 2000 U.S. Presidential race. For the most part American reporters tried to follow the brouhaha seriously with straight faces and ponderous tones. Not so the cartoonists and comedians around the world. The international reporters were giddy with delight because they didn't have to stretch or embroider any of it to get the laughs—all they had to do was tell it like it was.

In a country that had bragged about technological superiority for years the spectacle of faulty voting machines headed the list of election disasters. *Hanging Chads* became an overnight giggle phrase while poorly designed candidate lists on the machines repeatedly gave votes to the wrong people. Huge numbers of people weren't even allowed to vote because so many registrations were fouled up. Angry demonstrators marched around the streets calling for recounts and lawyers smacked their lips at the probability of court cases.

After a lot of grandstanding by both parties the decision of who did and who did not win was taken out of the hands of the people when the Republican head of the Florida Election Commission simply stated that George W. Bush had won and signed an 'official' document that said so. As predicted, the whole mess was then handed over to the lawyers. When the question got to the Supreme Court, the outcome was hardly a surprise, after all, the vote was destined to split along Conservative and Moderate/Liberal lines. The Court declared that there should be an immediate halt to the frantic recounting of ballots and announced the 'winner'. Final result? Georgie Porgie was said to be President. It didn't matter that the Florida vote was what gave him the edge in the Electoral College or that Al Gore had won the majority of the country's actual votes.

To an adult it was obvious that the election had been

stolen—it was also obvious that the smirking winners didn't care. The arrogance of the Brat out weighs even the tiniest need to feel shame. Consequently, it didn't take long for the new Administration to strut and flaunt as if it had been fairly elected. All of George's talk about being 'a uniter not a divider' went straight into the Oval Office wastebasket. Still angry over Bill Clinton's defeat of his father, his drubbing of Newt Gingrich's Congress and his avoidance of a real Impeachment, the new Prez wasted no time in paying back supporters with cushy appointments, government contracts and self-serving resolutions. For the childish, revenge is the sweetest of desserts.

When the American economy went *poof* after the attacks of 9/11, panic on Wall Street and in the corporate Board Rooms became the norm. How did the Polliwogs respond? They gave a huge tax cut to the rich. The old *Trickle Down* theory was dusted off and used as an excuse. That the TD theory had never worked in the past and was even less likely to work in the present was of no concern. Who cared if the little people got stiffed? Cutting taxes to benefit the wealthy could always be sold as 'being good for the economy'. And, since politics now runs on the money donated by the rich, it did not matter at all that the schedules making up the tax standards were heavily slanted in their favor even before the cuts.

Consider: People who earn less than $58,000 a year are taxed at a rate of 8% for Social Security while people who make more than that are taxed less and less until those with incomes of over $2,000,000. pay in a pitiful 1.66%. Do the math and you find that the lower income families tax rate is 4 ½ times higher than the rich while the rich families' income is a whopping 43 times greater. Just because it's called *Social Security* does not mean it is meant to secure the society. Tax benefits never trickle down, they soar up. The kiddies in charge make damn sure of it.

Adding to the problems facing the public is the deplorable fact that the Minimum Wage has not been raised in eight years. In 1997 it received a tiny boost to $5.15 an hour and it still sits there. During the 8 years of stagnation the purchasing power of the Minimum Wage has fallen 17% to put it at the second lowest level since 1955...a half century ago.

Remember also that at the same time the tax cut was pushed through Congress the airlines were bailed out of their pending collapses with tax payer money and the public was admonished to spend more. This was a public that was losing jobs by the multi-thousands every day while *The War On Terrorism* became the new political marketing slogan and was used to excuse all kinds of pork. Naturally, military spending shot off the charts.[3]

That many of the toys the warriors wanted were in no way connected to any kind of terror threat or war was conveniently ignored. A $24,000 sofa and armchair, a $1,800 pillow and $45,800 for fancy china and silver is not money spent to make people safer. Such purchases smell like the hard-core wastefulness of corporate shysters as does the Air Force's purchase of $53,000 golf carts, a $16,000 golf membership and $5,300 in golf club passes. When a label like *The War On Terrorism* is coined by politicians, it becomes the sheep's clothing for a lot of Big Bad Wolf decisions and when it emerged after 9/11 it became the number one reason for anything and everything that those in power wanted.

The Media knew that anything that criticized what was being done by the Administration would be frowned on as being unpatriotic. It was unpatriotic to mention that large government surpluses had disappeared over night through partisan spending. It was unpatriotic to mention any worry about the lack of funds for Social Security and Medicare and it was unpatriotic to question the emerging Energy Policy written by those who had been in the back pockets of the oil, gas and coal conglomerates for decades. The childish greed for power in politics is fed by even a whiff of war, so when the war on terror slogan lost some of its clout; when the corporate scandals finished busting the economy, the Administration had no hesitation in dreaming up another one. Suddenly there was the new battle cry about going to war in Iraq!

Turning a country's attention away from its economic misery with the trumpets of war is legitimate if there is a real and serious threat, but tootling those horns for political advantage is simply the Brat's way of sneaking out of trouble.

When President Bush spoke to the United Nations in September 2002 it was pretty clear he didn't want a peaceful solution to a situation that hadn't changed in 11 years. He wanted to pick a fight. Not only could he use it to sidestep the dismal economic numbers, he could rely on it to help his political cronies in the midterms in November. Saddam Hussein made a perfectly sound emotional target. Even so, the childishness shown by the Administration in its desire to send thousands of young men and women into a needless war while spending billions of taxpayer dollars to do so in order to pump up political advantage never would be allowed if adults were in charge.

Old news? No. Four years later over 2000 Americans have been killed, over 15,000 thousand more had been severely injured, multi-thousands of innocent Iraqi civilians are dead or destitute and there is no end in sight.

During the build up to the invasion the public had to search long and hard to find any media coverage of what the country and the world would be facing after a war. Once in a great while the potential problems were spelled out—as in Nicholas Kristof's column September 25, 2002 in the New York Times. Mr. Kristof was chillingly specific in pointing out that Iraq's 60% Shiite Muslim majority would love the chance to rebel against the Sunni majority. The last time that happened just after the Gulf War in 1991, the streets of Shiite cities like Karbala, Najaf and Basra ran red with the blood of Sunnis. Two weeks later Saddam brutally oppressed the rebellion while U.S. troops stood idly by. Kristof also addressed the potential problem with the Kurds in the north whose main city Kirkuk sits on a huge oil deposit. As of the summer of 2005 the continuous fighting was still going on and was still blamed on 'terrorists' with almost no analysis of the lack of solidarity in the population itself. It seems logical that the 'constitution' being argued over by every faction and ethnic grouping has almost no chance of really working.

While the war was advertised as being necessary in order to get rid of Hussein, the desire for Iraq's oil was kept as quiet as possible. Since the Administration was actively fighting even the most minor gas-conserving standards, it was not beyond a shadow of a doubt that oil was part and parcel of the plan.

The timing of the political battle babble was crucial. As elections drew nearer it was reported that over 2 million jobs had been lost since April 2001 and the numbers were still rising daily. As the midterms loomed on the immediate horizon polls showed that the public was twice as concerned about the economy as it was about any invasion of Iraq. The political landscape was still split right down the middle. Republicans hoisted the war club while Democrats pounded the economic drum. The real battle was going to be in the voting booth and neither side had a clear advantage.

One of the sacred traits of the Polliwog is the ability to play both sides of an issue at the same time. A stunning example is contained in the Bush Administrations double talk about where to drill for oil. First it pushed heavily for the right to drill in Alaska's Artic National Wildlife refuge. This was a rather obvious attempt at pay back for the political donations received by their pals in the energy business even though it would be a decade before any oil started flowing south and would only be enough to last about a year. Then in the hope of promoting the President's brother, Jeb Bush, in his second term run for Florida Governor, George W. allocated $255 million dollars in federal funds for a buy out against off shore drilling in the Everglades. With Congress pretty much guaranteed to approve the agreement $120 million would go to a family named Collier who 'owned' the rights. The second payment of $115 million could just be handed over to them since it didn't have to be approved by the legislators. The Bush brothers knew full well that since 73% of Floridians opposed off shore drilling, Jeb's campaign would get a positive kick. Brat flack at its best: we want to drill when it helps politically and we oppose drilling when it helps politically—such blatant scams fit right into the Pollwog cakewalk.

Mature thinking about any issue connected with an energy policy has never been part of the Administration's plans. One of the most scandalous fairy tales that was being written was authored by the supporters of the energy conglomerates that were appointed to or were behind the actions of the EPA and it political allies.[4] The first was a vote by the Senate in March of '02 to take off the table a bill to increase fuel standards for trucks and automobiles. By a margin of 62 to 38 the people's supposed advocates let the car companies, the oil companies and their dollar waving lobbyists continue to dictate what would and would not be allowed. It was no secret that the average fuel economy of the cars sold in 2001 was a pitiful 20.4 miles per gallon, the lowest and most wasteful in 22 years. The efficiency lost by not passing the bill would amount to roughly one million barrels of oil every day—interestingly the same amount imported from Kuwait and Iraq every twenty-four hours. As the gas prices rose to over $3 a gallon in the early fall of 2005 there was a sudden rush to look at the standards again and car companies suddenly started hyping the new hybrids as good buys. At the same time the cost of heating for the coming winter was expected to soar. The Brats suddenly got very quiet but they couldn't be expected to have changed their ways—they'll just wait for the next opportunity because when influence is bought it knows it will get the pay out. When heads of the big oil companies were called before Congress in November of 2005 to explain the huge profits they were raking in they defended their turf like true Brats. The possibility of facing a proposed 'profit tax" didn't even scare them…they knew they could depend on their political cronies to block it…and they did.

Normally the affects of cronyism are felt across the country but sometimes it has elements that impact foreign policy and inter-continental relationships. Such was the case when the Administration greased its political gears in states that rely on heavy manufacturing by arbitrarily imposing high tariffs on the importation of steel. No congressional approval was needed in order to give candidates a hefty boost for their rhetoric before the '02 midterms. The greed for immediate power totally over-ruled any concern for the almost certain disruption of friendly relations with European countries who would be certain to retaliate. Tomorrow's problems are never important to the childish.

The Brat's constant demand of "I want it now!" is illustrated graphically in the fight that goes on over the issue of Global Warming. The majority of the GOP side of the debate claims that there is evidence to support their claim that the planet is merely entering a 'natural' phase that occurs periodically and can't be accurately predicted or stopped. The other side maintains that the process, whether natural or not, is being speeded up and taken over by pollution caused by human activity. What's not talked about is that *even if* the first unlikely assertion is true, it doesn't make sense to add to the problem by ignoring the fact that human activity does make the situation worse. Since current political decisions are made by those in debt to the Money Bunnies who are at the top of the corporate polluter chain, every effort is made to let them keep operating as they do now. Even something so adult, so reasonable as private and public conservation, is looked at as being dangerous to the corporate energy demands. Vice President Dick Cheney was outraged when he barked that "conservation may be a sign of personal virtue" but that it was of little value to an energy policy. He was quite comfortable suggesting that such a 'virtue' was not worth even thinking about much less taking seriously.

Consider the impact on the process of potential environmental disasters by an early Bush nomination for the head of the now in-aptly named Clean Air Program — one Jeffrey Holmstead. Not only was Holmstead a lawyer for the Chemical Manufacturers Association, he was also the brains behind an anti-environmental group known as Citizens for a Sound Economy. An article published in the Pittsburgh Post-Gazette states positively that this group, the CRE, had "labeled most environmental problems—including acid rain, national resource depletion and shrinking landfill specs—as myths." Holmstead also represented agribusiness in a case challenging the effects of pesticide exposure on children. When the arrogance of childish behavior like that is allowed free rein, it is no surprise childish violence is the result. Who cares if the air that the children and adults are breathing is lethal and nothing is going to be done about it. But hey, what's the problem? It's just the peasants that are at risk.

It is a scientific fact that heat-trapping carbon dioxide gas stays in the air for a hundred years or more. Susan

Solomon, well known atmospheric scientist who works for the National Oceanic and Atmospheric Administration has calculated that humanity pumps 7 billions tons of carbon into the air every year or just about 20 trillion tons a day. Fossil fuel combustion and deforestation are the main sources. Even if all future emissions could be stopped it would take a century to reduce carbon dioxide to the levels of 1975. Still, that might turn out to be really good news for the gas mask manufacturers. One can always be optimistic when it comes to financial opportunities.

Childish violence is so much a way of life at the beginning of the 21st Century that it's hardly ever identified for what it is. In America the 'right to bear arms' is touted as a freedom granted to citizens by the Founding Fathers. That right, which originally was meant to be interpreted as a way to arm a militia in times of *national* need, is deliberately miss-stated or ignored by those who promote an increase in gun sales. Gun law reform comes up before legislators with predictable regularity and is shot down as quickly as it comes up. The National Rifle Association, the notorious NRA, spends big bucks to make sure that no real laws get passed— laws that would limit the manufacture, sales and collection of almost all types of shootin' arns…The cute little slogan 'Guns don't kill people, people do,' that the NRA uses to promote its platform naturally omits the obvious: people *with guns* kill. The sad irony of the fall 2002 rampage of serial killing up and down the highways in and around Washington D.C. was that they were done with high powered hunting rifles. While that may not be exactly the kind of hunting the NRA says it supports, it is one the Association and politicians must share some blame for, no matter who or what the cause. The murderers were caught, brought to trial and sentenced but that does not change the fact that it was incredibly easy for them to get the weapons and will stay that way since Congress passed another pro NRA resolution in the fall of 2005. Maybe the Representatives and the NRA biggies should play several rounds of that old favorite Russian Roulette...the last one standing gets to pay all the others' internment costs.

In the beginning the United States had no standing army or navy and was indeed dependent on its ordinary citizens for defense. Today the nation employs a variety of military branches as a permanent part of the Federal Government—as such, the Army, Navy, Air Force, Marine Corp, and the Coast Guard are formed under the auspices of the Pentagon and paid for by American taxpayers. While 'the people' may actually employ them, the activities that they may be ordered to take part in are designed and launched according to the desires of politicians—most directly the President and his Cabinet. When those in charge of the political agenda see war as a way to enhance or retain control, they have the power to send troops into situations that have no bearing whatsoever on the actual defense of the country. Political soapboxes are used to sell the ideas to the population, ideas that can lead to the death or injury of thousands—as in Iraq.

Keep in mind that those who do the selling never leave the comfort and safety of their own cushy homes and offices. Both the President and Vice President not only had rather questionable periods of military service but also a complete lack of battlefield experience. Both were on the front line of those hyping the need for war, advocating millions of dollars for military toys and calling those who cautioned restraint as cowardly and, of course, unpatriotic.

As stated, childish behavior is so much a part of the political framework that most of the time is goes unreported. Each of the two major political parties claims to be the true mirror of the nation's civic responsibility and design. The Republicans acknowledge that they represent the so-called conservative population, while the Democrats waver between being edgy and comfortable about anything called liberal. The GOP has it easy since a major component of the conservative mindset is that it is always and forever right. In such a setting it is no trouble for the party and its spokespeople to blame anyone who disagrees with them for all kinds of misjudgments and to paint them as evil.

On the other side of the aisle the Democrats have a much harder road to travel because liberal intelligence acknowledges that everyone is entitled to his or her own views and that one is not necessarily better or more 'right' than the other. What's not mentioned is that with this kind of *liberal* thinking the Republicans have a built in advantage—being 'right' is a ploy that evokes emotion and emotion sells. Whenever Democrats try to get an issue debated in logical, intellectual terms they are drowned out by partisan hysteria. It is a no win situation. If they lose their tempers and respond in combative tones, they are immediately labeled as being partisan and unwilling to work together for the good of the country. If they don't get riled up, they're called wishy washy and ineffective. Brat tactics can sit on both sides of the fence with ease.

Response to an emotional outburst is childish if it's what is used to make a decision. In politics the deliberate use of emotion to get one's way can be one of the most childish of all tactics and when the emotion being used is childishly nasty, it becomes the accepted methodology for winning.

When the Presidential Campaign started heating up early in '04 it was interesting and attention getting to see that, against all odds, the Democrats came out swinging and not at each other but at the Republicans. They were taking seriously the fact that they represented half of the American people and that their half was livid about almost everything the GOP was doing. It was clear that the gloves were off.

Unfortunately, we must always remember that it has become impossible for the citizen to know what goes on behind the closed doors of politics. It's increasingly difficult to have enough honest information to make good decisions about what the government should and shouldn't be doing. Because the political animal is joined at the hip with the corporate beast that multi-legged mammoth has a tight grip on what people hear.

Nothing could illustrate that more clearly than the flap in the 9/11 Commission hearings that erupted near the end of March '04. While the panel was evenly divided between party reps, who all piously had maintained that their proceedings were being conducted on a non-partisan playing field, the appearance of ex-terrorist honcho Richard Clarke threw that nonsense right down the D.C. sewer. Up until that day, the hearings had puttered along with rather rag tag and minimum coverage by the media that chose to maintain that the hearings were really only highly important to the survivors and friends and relatives of those killed. There had been one little squeak over the airwaves when the Committee asked for more time and the Administration tried to deny the request and then backed down because of the sudden coverage. Other than that, the public didn't really hear much about what was going on during the many months of the panel's investigation.

Clarke's approaching session suddenly was heralded with complete media fan fare the week before his appearance as he was interviewed and photographed by everyone who could get within shouting distance. Part of the chatter concerned his new book that dealt with his time as an anti-terrorist expert and part was about his very recent resignation from his post in the Bush Administration. It was stated over and over that he had been an insider in presidential circles for 30 years—all the way back to Ronnie Reagan.

When Clarke sat down and took the oath in front of the Committee on Wednesday, March 24th, every news channel in the country ran continuous, non-interrupted coverage. The build up had been so intensely pursued, including an interview with Leslie Stahl on *60 Minutes* just a few days before his appearance, that the media was sure that millions of viewers would tune in. And they were right and it was worth it!

Besides his lengthy testimony that illustrated how the Bush Administration had deliberately ignored the possibility of terrorist attacks before 9/11, two things in Clarke's recital were completely unusual for any current government spokesperson or agency: first he actually apologized for failing at his job. Second, he said that the continuous positive spin put on reports coming out of the White House, by him and others, was a matter of politics, not morality. For once a member of the political elite responded to an event like an adult.

When the White House responded to questions concerning his statements it more or less had to resort to name calling and finger pointing as it tried to discredit the man who had advised Presidents for three decades. Besides, they knew they could just wait it out since 'The Media' would quickly move to another story. Sadly, they were right and it did.

We know that by the beginning of the 21st Century the dissemination of information was tightly controlled by The Money Bunnies and The Polliwogs and the other member of the three-legged mammoth **The Quackers**. Known in modern slang as *The Media*, it benefited from and enhanced the power of the triumvirate to a level never imagined and will continue to do so as long as it is in the tight grip of corporate power. All Hail the Mighty Ducks of the world's communication systems.

CHAPTER 3

The Quackers

Information and Communication

It might seem with modern technology and the instant availability of information that people have a better chance of knowing what's going on in the world. Theoretically, that could be true, unfortunately...it most certainly is not. Why? Because every bit of gabble that's reported is in every form of the media slanted, from its very beginning. The viewer, the listener or reader is constantly at the mercy of **The Quackers**—the broad billed, feather brained ducks that childishly control all forms of communication. The *spin* that we identified is now a basic programmed part of all reporting. So basic is it that the thinking individual simply takes it for granted.

First and foremost, political informants are expected

to say only that which puts their side in the best light. What's not expected, or even thought about, is that everything that's seen, heard or read has a deliberate slant or spin—it's simply the nature of the game. Many people are indeed aware that the information providers are controlled by mega corporations but not many are consciously skeptical about the amount of influence those companies are wielding on a daily basis. Suffice it to say that absolutely nothing goes over the air or into print that can have any type of negative impact on the bottom line of the corporations that, quite literally, *own* the news. Nothing is allowed to jeopardize the flow of dollars coming in and those in charge will consciously and knowingly favor those who provide it.

When we talk about communication we need to remember that we are a species that makes and uses symbols *for* communication. Most of us take this for granted and never stop to consciously think about what this means. We don't look at the fact that ideas cannot be formed, shared or put to work without the symbols that express them. And, as a 'thinking' species we are not conscious of the amazing reality that every single thing, whether physical or imagined, in our personal and public environment, everything is represented as a symbol. In other words, the sky, the car, the dream, the tree, the cat, the fork, the self are all just symbols...symbols and *only* symbols. Specific as well as emotional meanings attached to symbols can and do vary wildly from person to person yet there has developed a consensus that seems to say that intercommunication is not just possible but easy. It's not!

The more modern we think ourselves the more we

seem to ignore the changes going on as our creation of and dependence on symbols gets ever more complicated and arcane. We move farther and farther away from really understanding them and each other. Accordingly, language—words, definitions and combinations—is a process that is constantly in a state of upheaval that few people really can identify.

The study of Latin and Greek, the seeds of a lot of western language, disappeared from public schools decades ago so that today many of the words and phrases used have colloquial meanings that are in total opposition to their origins.

For those who study the elements of communication, the public's lack of knowledge can sometimes provide a delicious private snicker. Consider the word nice that is so sickeningly repeated in the phrase "Have a nice day." What people don't know is that nice comes from Old French, was pronounced *nee-say* and originally meant *ignorant!*[1] Hilarious and sadly appropriate that millions of us are wishing each other a dumb day and don't even know it.

From an adult point of view it is also sad that today's idea of good communication is based on speed rather than clarity. While this reality is seen and bragged about in connection with the world of the Internet, it is also true in that of the press whether it be in the form of television, radio or in print. Accuracy has given way to the need to be first. One of the more vividly idiotic and truly childish examples was seen when the verdict from Martha Stewart's trial for lying about a stock sale was aired.

Every network and cable channel had cameras and reporters camped *en masse* outside the courthouse.

Stooges inside were primed to alert them immediately after the verdict was read. Each crew was placing its 'reporting' skill on the line as it tried to be first to say whether the jury had said guilty or innocent. The resulting mess looked more like a scene from *Saturday Night Live* rather than a story that was hyped as important news. The stampede of characters that came bursting out of the hallowed halls of law practically started a riot as reporters scuffled for the Blue Ribbon Win. And what a win it would be since the event was simultaneously being aired across every major outlet — a win of maybe 2 whole seconds? Did they at least all get it right? Of course not, one ducky equipped with a large paper score sheet and big magic markers checked a square labeled 'innocent', was yelled at, showed his confusion in front of the cameras and finally corrected his mistake to 'guilty'. Trying to be first has become such a constant media contest that the viewer forgets how childishly silly it really is.

As shown by the Martha Megathon, the conglomerate known as The Media has the capacity to invade the lives of even the most reluctant viewer and constantly uses this overwhelming power to its own best advantage. Since the information entities owe their existence to the advertisers, the formula breaks down to dollars before it even begins to consider communication. When the population gets its information from sources dedicated to airing only that which is deemed profitable, the info isn't just warped, it's basically worthless.

Knowing that the easiest way to avoid having to deal with serious issues is to trivialize everything, all of The Quackers have become geniuses at the art of *twaddle*. It's no secret that the TV box spews almost constant drivel. It starts in the morning with the numerous yakkity blabs that pretend to be Informational Talk Shows. Unless there is a national catastrophe like the hurricanes Katrina and Rita the high profile hosts and hostesses spend about two minutes on national and world event headlines for every twenty minutes of interviews with the likes of movie idols, sports figures and people who star in other productions made by the same network or channel. The self-advertising is constant. Not caring whether what's heard is meaningful, helpful or even true, The Media focus is on whatever keeps the money flowing in. If the provider can get more people to watch its other programs, the dollar signs add up to more than those for the competition.

A public that has been conditioned to believe that 'sound bites' can actually reflect what is happening now mindlessly over looks contradictions in what is aired.

For example, it is not a hidden fact that the *News* side of corporate television has no trouble showing politicians and religious tub-thumpers bemoaning a lack of sexual morals in America while its advertisers use lewd images to sell everything from cars to soda pop. The beer commercials are particularly double sided when the same company can sanctimoniously lecture about the danger of driving while under the influence—a slogan that means *drunk*—at the same time it is running bawdy ads set in bars. The net result is that the country's prudish pilgrimism has no trouble existing with its thirst for decadence. Both attitudes can be tapped for money; both are happily used without even a hint of shame because when the Brats are in control they have no qualms about making the increase in income the only criteria. The pious beer ads are specifically designed to hook drinkers of 40 years and older to a particular brand, at the same time the sexy ones target young guzzlers for the exact same make of bubbly. The process makes sure that The Quackers can afford to toast each other in champagne.

Not satisfied with the amount of money coming in from schedules for advertising that were loosely established over a span of many years, the number of minutes allotted has lately been rising steadily. It was reported in MindShare, a company that monitors programming on network TV's big four—ABC, CBS, NBC and Fox—that the average *clutter* of 14.27 minutes per hour recorded in 2001 had gone to over 15 minutes by 2005 and was still climbing. *Clutter* is defined as advertising as well as network and local affiliate self-promotion. However even if the viewer has a fast finger on the remote and is an adept surfer, it doesn't do any good because the clutter is synchronized across all stations. It's best to just hit the mute, or blab off button.

Often the onslaught of gabble is referred to as a 'Commercial Break'. These often come before and after an excitedly hyped 'Breaking News' report that may or may not deal with anything worth hearing and is run over and over during the entire day to try and entice viewers to stay with the same network or channel. The practice of continuously repeating the same news during a day's broadcasting is only one method of trivialization. The other is the practice of reporting an event not just for days, but also for weeks, or months, or years. The Jon Benet Ramsey case was a perfect example of that type of saturation. People felt sorry for the little girl and sincerely hoped that some sort of justice would be done but they also got tired of the endless coverage that was still being brought up eight years after the child's death.

The same was true for the Clinton/Whitewater/MonicaLewinsky/Impeachment nonsense. True the series of stories was propelled by political mania and fanaticism, but The Media played right into it and was tipsy with delight at being able to continuously report something that *sounded like news*. Considering the non-stop coverage of those monumentally idiotic events, it is interesting that the public is still told by The Media that *The Media* is in the grip of demonic Left Wing Liberals. If that is true, pray tell how it is that the Conservative Right Wingers dominate all forms of airtime?

Easy…the practice continues to grow in Quacker acceptance because the whole of the information process is owned by big corporations that totally lean toward the Republican views about the sanctity of business and its right to do whatever it pleases to increase its wealth. Without any shame whatsoever, the Brats in charge put people on camera who reflect their own bias at the same time they are lamenting that the opposing side is to blame for whatever it is they're yapping about. When the childish use the idea of always being right to further their agenda, the public doesn't stand a chance of hearing anything being dealt with in an adult fashion.

As we've said, the fact that the corporate world lives and dies by a total commitment to greed is not a secret. Nor is it a hidden fact that greed has become so common as a desired way of life that it is the basic element of The American Dream. Endless advertising in favor of it has so changed people's views that merely having enough to live decently is no longer a satisfying goal. The public is constantly told that it must want more of everything — more money, more fluff and more stuff. In that kind of atmosphere it is not too surprising that the corporate scandals that rocked the country's economy did not in any way change the theme. If anything, it simply upped the volume and the saturation point of advertising as companies fought over the little money and/or credit the general population had left.

It also was stressed in shows that were developed to high light how wonderful greed could be. A game show actually called *Greed* hit the air and didn't cause a single blip of negative comment. That it didn't last very long was a result of being poorly designed, not because it sent a nasty message. In fact, all it did was set off a rash of programs based on greed. The celebrated *Who Wants To Be A Millionaire?* hit the Neilson Chart with a bang and stayed at the top for several very profitable years and brought in many more millions than it was paying out. When viewers' response finally waned it went to a five-days-a-week afternoon format with a pretty hostess instead of the older more 'intellectually' posed Regis Philbin. Still, it had been such a money pot, maybe it could be squeezed again...sure. Early in 2004 it was decided to plop the cherry on the top of the yummy corporate concoction by introducing a special weekly show that brought back Regis and raised the top prize to $10 million. That was so profitable — no one won the 10 mil — that it was announced it would be repeated sometime in the future. What should not be taken lightly is that the arena of information and communication is not about either — it is about making money.

The holiest of all corporate mandates reads like a Commandment: *Thou shall cut costs at all costs.* In television that means a continuous search for types of shows that look spectacular but can be produced on a relatively small budget. Gotta give 'em credit for doing the job well with the creation of the achingly-long-running and stunning leader of smarmy—*Survivor.* Promoted as a 'reality' experience, the first example of that outdoor farce had 16 people dumped on a little island to compete for...yep...$1 million. As the show progressed with once a week airings an entire range of childish traits was used by the producers to make sure the contestants fought each other for the prize. It worked well. The participants were urged to cooperate and betray each other at the same time, to actively try to be in control of the whole situation and to lie, cheat and steal in the effort to win. The title was a double meaning joke that implied an atmosphere of danger that did not exist. Being the Survivor was about one kid taking all the toys away from the others and had nothing to do with real safety. A person is not stranded or in much danger when being constantly interviewed, photographed and hustled from one contrived activity to another.

True to form, however, the audiences slurped up the Brat antics and the creators laughed all the way to the bank. It was such a cash register success that it goes on...and on...and on...Competing networks constantly try to come up with an idea that can compete for the *Survivor* audiences and the loot it generates. If they could somehow steal the whole gimmick they would be happy to do so—stale bread on the corporate pond is good food for The Quackers. If it's pre-digested, so much the better.

NBC began battling valiantly with a show called *Fear Factor* that did come across as a goofy spin off but it wasn't good enough. The network made up for it with a canny display of childishness in the workplace when it concocted *The Apprentice*. An audience smash from the beginning with its contestants vying for a job with 'The Donald' by using all the traits of the Brat and, at times, coming up with new ones of their own. The prize in that is a one-year job that pays a pitiful $250,000 while Mr. Trump gets a guaranteed fee of 1 million per episode. As always, the ads sold for each production pay for it and his little palm greasing without a hiccup.

Even with such a display of blatant nonsense the reality shows are not really any more contrived than the so-called news coverage and when the two can be linked, it's pure gravy. Consider *The Apprentice* spin off that featured Miss Martha and began soon after she got out of jail and home confinement. Now she could play fuzzy wuzzy about her homemakers' advice while picking a contestant who gets a job at her company. Trump complained that Martha was taking viewers away from his show while both showed a slow down in popularity. By mid November '05, NBC Stewart's was dumped after one little run.

It should be clear by now that the 'need' for news is about 10% real and about 90% contrived. It is helpful to know, for example, if there is a sudden contamination of the city's drinking water or if there is a nutcase walking around without his pants on. What's not helpful is to have the talking heads going on for hours about things like the history of the contamination of H_2o in the U.S. or a long dissertation about bare bottoms but that's usually the type of 'follow up' one is forced to mute. The Quackers honestly believe that a made up story is just as good as a real one and who's going to know the difference anyway? After all, it's all theater and it does not matter if the sets, the actors and the lines they quote are as phony as anything seen on a real stage.

As the year 2004 began to take shape, the opportunities for News in America, real or not, swept into high gear with the upcoming Presidential Election and the continuation of the mess surrounding the military action in Iraq. For the first few months the Democratic Primaries gave the outlets constant ammunition for hours and hours of political honking. Debates among candidates were seen as perfect little passion plays that then could be chewed on endlessly by both Democratic and Republican duckbills. For a while the biggest story was how Governor Howard Dean of Vermont was changing the political process by his campaign's smart use of the Internet and its ability to bring young people to the table. It was therefore a stunning surprise to a lot of the pundits when Dean lost in Iowa and his rival, John Kerry, suddenly became the hot topic.

And on top of the unexpected results and besides the political meaning of the votes, The Quackers were handed a 24/7 news leader with what was immediately labeled *The Scream*. Whatever his motives might have been in giving that speech after his loss, Dean fell flat on his keester with the yell heard around the world. For weeks every report of the debates, the caucuses and primaries also included The Scream and commentary as to whether it was or wasn't the reason howling Howard had begun an avalanche of losses. By the time Senator

Kerry had sewed up the Democratic nomination, Dean was long gone and yet The Scream was still heard echoing off the canyon walls of media coverage. Still, the fight had really just begun. There were eight months to go before the national election so the reporting of the battle began in earnest and promised to provide lip-smacking fodder for the duckies dedicated to filling the air with political puffery.

If we take into consideration the many years we have been in existence, we see that the *idea* of The News hasn't been a part of our lives for very long. In our youth we were only concerned with what was happening is our own tiny clan, tribe or settlement. The 'news' of those who belonged to the communities was all that mattered and was simply the daily gossip. As our numbers grew and we built villages and towns to cater to the surrounding farmers, word was still passed back and forth among neighbors and local traders. The talk was what we now call 'folksy' and dealt with intimate issues — who had a baby, who died, how the crops were doing and what the weather was going to be like next month. In those days we didn't know *where* we were or how big the lands around us were.

Later as our groupings got bigger and were headed by kings or chieftains, we stretched out and explored. We found there were other people who had different ideas and different ways of doing things. There were people who wanted to be friendly and people who didn't and we started the verbal and physical clashes that have grown into the inter-national and inter-ethnic wars of today.

It would be wise of us to remember, however, that for a very long time the news still was not something the average bloke cared about. If he wasn't forced to slog off and fight for his village or leader, he stayed in the same small community all his life. Later, if a little country was at war with a neighbor, the locals got word of events from returning warriors or from those who came to take the crops and animals to supply the troops. If they were friendly troops, people simply suffered from starvation, if they were enemy soldiers, the people were murdered or hauled off as slaves. Nevertheless, it was all still just a pattern of tiny fusses on a very small playing field.

Our isolation from each other was a global way of life for most of the planet for century after century. Even in the days of the early empires the average peasant didn't know or care what was going on outside his own little territory. People were actually taught to be suspicious of strangers and their stories and often simply did not believe what they were told about other customs or cultures. And for nearly all of those centuries news was still only heard by way of mouth.

Yes, we did concoct a number of ingenious forms of writing thousands of years ago, but the common squiff had no idea what the squiggles meant and he couldn't take time to care because life was too hard and too short to worry about such nonsense. In ancient Egypt the peasant, the aristocracy and most of the Pharaohs couldn't read the hieroglyphics on the tombs and monuments any more than we can. Those skills were the sole responsibility of a special class called scribes and they were part of the culture in Egypt, China, Japan, and some of the early empires in the Middle East like Babylon and Ur. Today it is the religious inscriptions that are most well known to the casual history buff but even then most of the writing had to do with economics—how much grain the Pharaoh had left after the last war and where the Imperial Emperor's sake and jade was being stored. It wasn't called the economy then but it was thought to be the most important part of all the countries development.

In spite of that, artisans all over the planet were also quite creative in figuring out how to record those things that were emotionally critical to them and their people. From the Inca of Peru to the Vikings of the northern lands, pieces of art made from every conceivable material were created in a wondrous variety of forms...and each used our old friends the *symbols* to depict its message. The meanings of most of them died when the culture was conquered or faded away and the ones that survived destruction and time had to be re-interpreted centuries later when it was finally deemed okay to look into the past from a non-finite viewpoint. It took a long time for us to come to that decision because the western world was under the thumb of religious fanatics for so many years.

It's a well-documented fact that in the aptly named Dark Ages much of the population was afraid of writing because they were constantly told that it was the work of The Devil. What a perfect example of our use of childish power to cement control—the Bible was The Word of God but any other document came from Satan. Not surprisingly most of the aristocracy of The Middle Ages, which were of course still Dark, couldn't read anymore than their early Egyptian counterparts.

Gradually after the printing press was invented more of us learned to read, to cipher numbers and to study things that were far away. The idea, however, that it might be beneficial for all of a population to have some sort of formal education is an incredibly recent concept. Such a program does, after all, carry a potential danger to those in power. An educated populace might actually be able to intellectually challenge the motives and actions of the top Brats.

They needn't fear too much in our hotsy totsy modern society—with the Quackers as a part of their clique not much of importance is read about by today's' peasants.

For the childish, power over others gives a sense of security. For the mature, that kind of power is known to be the most dangerous. It is dangerous to individuals, to families, societies and humanity as a whole. Controlling what people know is now one of the most blatant examples of the misuse of power over others and it is chillingly horded in the hands of a very few individuals.

In recent decades as the use of radio and the newspapers waned, television began to consolidate its firm grip on the information made available to the public and when cable was first introduced it took a while for it to erode some of the communication monopoly held by the old fashioned networks. As more and more channels exploded across the screen, ABC, NBC and CBS began to merge with other media heavies or even totally unrelated but wealthy corporations to counteract the rising competition. And, as always, when the rule of the lowest common denominator kicked in, they all began to sound alike. Also it must be stated as a matter of national concern that the idea that what they report is censored is a question those at the top refuse to answer.

A tiny little piece of coverage after hurricane Katrina gives a direct and correct response to that question even if its brief airing was considered a mistake by those in charge.

On one of his later trips to New Orleans, George W. was surveying the situation where the pumping of the liquid from the broken dikes had been underway for a few days. As usual he was surrounded by a mob of reporters and cameramen who jostled and pushed trying to get their questions to him and have his answers recorded.

One asked: "How do you think it's going, Mr. President?"

Bush replied: "I think the *de-watering* is going well."

This little exchange was shown in an early morning news segment and—as far as can be told, it was never aired again. The White House handlers got to the head of the stations in a flash and that telling little bit of fluff was edited out of each and every clip that showed his visit to the city. Because it was done so quickly and efficiently, it would be hard to prove that it ever was said but out in the land there are thousands of people who know for sure that it was. Whether admitted or not, that kind editing is censorship. If something so inane, so silly really, is considered dangerous to those in control, take a deep breath and think for a moment about what else is being erased.

An adult knows that there is a basic difference between being intelligence and being shrewd. Intelligence uses critical, i.e. questioning, thinking to find out about something. Shrewdness looks for cracks in the person's or process' armor to criticize in order to gain an edge over any potential rival. The things being criticized do not have to be true in order to be used for that advantage.

Sadly, all of the television providers got a much-needed veneer of legitimacy as they shrewdly reported the September 11th attacks and the following fury and compassion of the American public. Starting that morning when the first tower of The World trade Center was hit, *The Media* swung into instant and constant reporting. That people were is shock was obvious; that they would be glued to their screens was certain. This, for once, was really *News*!

If and when one can study the whole horrible situation objectively, it must be realized that just because the ongoing events that were reported concerning the aftermath of the high jacked planes was real and serious, it did *not* mean any change in media control. If anything, the desire for control got heavier. With such a full slate of mind blowing reports and images that the people really cared about, the fight to see whose network or channel would draw the most viewers began in earnest and very quickly resembled a shark feeding frenzy.

The stories were carefully divided between patriotic hype, valiant attempts at rescue and pictures that focused on the sorrow and sadness of citizen death. Reporters knew that the outpouring of sympathy for the families and friends of those killed was real because they were simply innocents who were in the wrong place at the wrong time. They also knew that the emotions, though real, were really, really good theater. What the viewers forgot in a time of crisis is that theater is what sells and what sells is what runs the machines that control what is seen. Though there were few breaks and almost no advertising, the stations counted on the fact that a pleased audience would come back to them in more normal times.

In times of national upheaval *The Media* is the most powerful arm of any government. It is used to convince the public that what is being done is what needs to be done. Under its umbrella all sorts of political and military nonsense can be sold and implemented in the name of patriotism. In such times any and all criticism can be called anti-American, subversive and a threat to national safety. With the amiable cooperation of The Quackers, The Polliwogs are given free rein to do exactly as they please.

As the weeks and months passed after the attacks, it was interesting to see how the press bought into the constant propaganda of patriotic blather. Every time there was even a hint of disapproval, government and military icons would call a 'briefing' to defend the rightness of their decisions. The staged productions were carried by each and every major news outlet and then endlessly 'interpreted' by the studios' talking ducks. Yes, there were important things going on both at home and abroad, and yes, citizens were very interested in what was happening. What the citizens didn't need was to be told that they had to give blanket approval to schemes and actions that they would rightfully shoot down in a New York minute if they were really allowed to be aware of what was going on.

The childishness of the grab for total control exhibited by those at the top set the stage for much, much more of the same in the coming years. At the end of '05 the grab was still their major focus of attention.

The Brats attention would not be diverted, but they loved it when the populations could be side tracked. With instant coverage and multiple channel opportunities available it has become easy to do. For example, in a majority of countries *Sports* is one of the most valuable diversions ever invented. Today those in power use it exactly like the old Roman Coliseum contests that were staged to keep people's minds off of what the Emperors and Senators were doing. Now sporting events have taken on enormous importance as mental sleeping pills. With the constant broadcast of games, tournaments and play-offs, the couch potato is not too likely to care about anything but his teams and their performances on the field.

While there has always been a loose tie between sports and nationalism the patriotic spectacles flaunted before and during games after 9/11 became huge. Firefighters and policemen from New York were standard guests in stadiums all around the country. Some of them carried mammoth American flags around the fields while others were just shown on camera for the national audience. Dignitaries, including President Bush, threw out the 'first' ball before the World Series of 2001. Mayor Guilliani was present wearing a Yankee's cap and people were shown crying during the playing of the National Anthem.

The fact that the biggest loss of life had been in New York and it was its team that was trying to repeat as baseball's World Champions made the whole thing very touching. The politicians and *The Media* sat up and took notice...sports had become the most useful venue for patriotism and certainly the most lucrative. Advertisers fell over each other trying to create commercials that tied their products to blaring statements of pride for America. Sports had absolutely nothing to do with the attacks but it was a marvelous vehicle for keeping attention on them. Liking and being interested in a sport is not necessarily childish. Becoming totally absorbed by it is.

If there ever was any doubt in the minds of adult news viewers that there was a direct link connecting The Polliwogs and The Quackers it could be laid to rest early in 2005. To the skeptic, however, it didn't come as a big surprise or shock when it was discovered that one Armstrong Williams, a conservative commentator, was paid a nifty $241,000.00 to tout the Bush education initiative called No Child Left Behind. Mr. Williams tried to defend the pay off by saying he supported the program even before he was paid...read bribed...for praising it. After all, if the news is intended to help those in power sell their views what's wrong with helping those who help? The story was featured in editorial and Op Ed pages, on talk shows and prime time reporting but the number of days it took to see it completely disappear from all outlets could be counted on one half of one hand. No surprise there—feeding the ducks is simply a routine process no matter what ethical meanies might say.

While there is not much room for optimism concerning the direction in which all forms of communication are going, there is one tiny bright light in the middle of that big dark tunnel. It is a half hour show broadcast on Comedy Central that has swept the plate clean of television garbage, called *The Daily Show* with masterful host Jon Stewart and a power packed crew of writers and actors, it boasts about airing *fake* news. The program rattles national and international events so beautifully it won Peabody Awards for Stewart in '04 and '05! The most heartening aspect of its soaring success is that it draws a huge crowd of loyal viewers from the country's youth while also appealing to a lot of their parents and grandparents. The program does such a good job of showcasing the nonsense going on in Washington, around the country and around the world, that there are actually people now who are beginning to understand some of our problems. It is to be hoped that it has a long and happy run since its *fake* news tells what's really going on so much better than any of the supposedly real media outlets.

In closing, the word *media* is worth a quick peek…Most people don't see that it's simply the plural of the word *medium* and so is supposed to be a definition of the process. Therefore, *The Media* is a group of *mediums* by which the *medium* of communication is deployed. How's that for a thigh slappin' Quack?

CHAPTER 4

The Lardbutters

Religion

While the Brats that make up the ranks of The Polliwogs are known for their oily ways no group of humanity's top bellowing blowhards can spread the grease like **The Lardbutters** that are the self proclaimed autocrats of our species infamous religions. They constantly test the old maxim that 'oil and vinegar don't mix' by promising buttery redemption if you believe and do what they say while screaming acidic damnation if you don't.

Thousands and thousands of years ago when we first began making stone axes to kill animals for food and each other for fun, it made some sense to think that there was some kind of clan of *spirits* who were in charge of things.

It was a big scary world out there with big scary events just waiting to happen. Since it was so big and we were so few, we didn't see much of each other and spread out as we were over the many inhabitable miles of land, it was easy to come up with a variety of inventions to try and explain the forces of nature and each other. And, since we thought, and wanted to think, that we were the smartest of all beings, we egotistically began to proclaim that those spirits were like us…only more so.

Not surprisingly, the struggle for power began immediately. In some tribes and clans the secular leader, the practical chieftain, was also the spiritual leader but in most the duties and responsibilities were split and the childish battle for supremacy was thus initiated around the world. Over the millennia it has grown and intensified and now is a basic reason for the religious wars of the 21st Century. The autocrats of the major and minor religious congregations are still fighting for the ultimate in power and like the true Brats they are, show no signs of even slowing down much less stopping.

When the growth of religious awareness is shown through the common beliefs of its historical roots some amusing, and also troubling, clerical fundamentals can be put into perspective. Until very, *very* recently humanity did not even question the idea that the earth was flat. It was a *known fact* and was accepted without even a hint of doubt. Yes, the land had its mountains and valleys but it was flat—we walked on it and that proved it!

When you teach that the earth is really a big pancake it's not hard to also decide that *up* is good and *down* is bad. And in that framework you can put the good spirits—now called 'gods' by many different groups—above the flapjack in a pretty place and the bad ones in a nasty one below where the natural eruption of volcanoes led to the description of a fiery hell. Those who claimed to talk to the gods detailed at great length and in stupefying precision the elements of those domains as they used them with fanatic assurance to make people think and act in accordance with the current teachings of the local organization.

After thousands of years, a few people began to think for themselves; to ask questions and to look for answers based on what was to become known as *science*. When the idea of the flat earth was finally debunked it took a long time for the explanation to take hold because it was so vigorously damned from the pulpit. Science proved, rather easily considering the feeble tools it had to work with at the time, that the earth was round, its moon was round and that the eight other bright stars in the sky were also round and should now be called planets...planets that satirically are still named for ancient gods.

There followed some nasty dust ups concerning the idea that the earth was or was not the center of The Universe and those led to even more historically significant fights between science and religion. At the risk of underlining the obvious, it might be pointed out that in the end Science won all of them. It is now taken as truth that our sun is a hot star in the middle of our galaxy that all the planets, including ours, orbits and that gravity is a reality that manifests because of the orbiting. The system works beautifully but, incidentally, makes the whole concept of *up* and *down* a simple matter of local definition.

On the comical side of things, science could even be said to be able to take a stand if comparing the ancient religions with the so-called modern ones. The old ones saw energy and the spirit of consciousness in everything—the trees, the water, the air, the plants, the animals and in important events and actions. Each had its own god or goddess and was worshipped in his or her temple. The deities of War were at odds with the deities of Peace, the spirits of the forest lived in or among the trees and the deities of Life and Death decided who would live and who would die as well as where and when and how. Today it is scientifically known that there is, indeed, energy and subatomic levels of consciousness in everything. So much for the *pagans* being stupid...they were closer to the truth thousands of years ago than the religions of the modern age are today. All Hail the Roman god of dung, *Stercutius*, he would fit right in today.

When we fast-forward to the idiocy of the religions of our time we find that nothing has really changed from the Dark Ages. Today the three self proclaimed main religions—the Christian, Islamic and Jewish—are at each other's pious throats with the same kind of venom and hate they spewed at each other two thousand years ago. The only discernable difference is that now they have modern weapons with which to kill each other and whoever else might get in the way. In the past, thousands of innocents were slain in the name of a god; in the present, thousands of innocents are slain in the name of a god. Why? Altogether now: Power and Control.

With that in mind, the last thing the Lardbutters want to do is modernize their organizational rituals or icons and they certainly do not want any of their beliefs questioned. If an old manuscript that was cobbled together over hundreds years says that a god created the world in six days a mere three thousand years ago, then anything that Science says that is different is just plain wrong. Never mind that Archeology, Astronomy, Biology and Nuclear and Quantum Physics have tons of verifiable proof to the contrary. People are still taught that spirits called angels fly around in an 'atmospheric heaven' with wings and that the so-called heaven and hell are up and down. Even the details haven't changed from the Flat Earth days—the upper region has clouds and is entered through a gate while the lower is filled with fire. The power of the suet that is shoveled is truly amazing and is bought unthinkingly by billions of poor monkey see, monkey do followers of each form of religion.

A nasty battle that illustrates the egotism of the Brat in church clothing is the one played out for a number of years at the Air Force Academy in Colorado Springs, Colorado. To begin with we must remember that the United States Air Force is a branch of the country's military organization that is run by the government and paid for by citizen taxes. As part of that complex, its official training school, The Academy, is bound by the same criteria as any other nationally supported institution. Under those rules it must follow the stipulations of the Constitution, treat all people fairly and live by a pronounced code of ethics. By the spring of 2004 it became public that a lot of those rules weren't just being bent, they were being ripped to shreds and dumped in the garbage.[1]

By the use of a current law, an investigation was initiated to check out rumors that cadets at the school were being subjected to heavy Christian evangelical proselytizing. The study went on for over a year and enough was found early on for the school to have to agree to reforms. Not much changed, however, as seen when in June of '05 the Superintendent, Lt. General John Rosa, Jr., was quoted as saying that the problem of cadets being unfairly pressured to adopt Christian beliefs and practices was still going on. "Perception is reality" the General declared in reference to the many complaints that the cadets' constitutional rights had been violated by the militant evangelicals who used peer pressure and did so with the approval of authority figures in the chain of command.

Not only did General Rosa have to reprimand his Second in Command, a born again Christian, for being part of the scheme, he acknowledged that a campus Chaplin went so far as to warn hundreds of cadets that those not 'born again' would "burn in the fires of hell".

Not only had nothing changed or been 'reformed', Superintendent Rosa said it would probably take as long as six years to fix the mess...and it wasn't going to help the process that a Captain, Lutheran Chaplin Melinda Morton, who had dared complain had been transferred to Asia by The Air Force. In true Brat fashion when the brass at the top saw that her testimony was potentially damaging, they simply removed her. A tiny notice in the back pages of some newspapers announced that Chaplin Morton had been recalled for questioning but no major coverage mentioned her at all.

With so many dead ends in sight one could hardly

blame General Rosa when he announced that in the fall of '05 he would leave the Academy and take over as the head of The Citadel, another well-known military school in South Carolina. Who knows whether his replacement will have the guts to act with real honesty and concern for the welfare of the cadets and time may or may not tell because The Lardbutters hadn't given up and were busily prodding members of congress to get further involved. By the third week of October 2005, dozens of Congressional Representatives were drafting a letter to the President that would ask him to produce an executive order to protect 'free speech' for military chaplains. As of Friday the 21st 58 members of the governing body had signed the letter which stated: "Christian military chaplains are under direct attack and their right to pray according to their faith is in jeopardy."

The childish bickering went all the way to the United States Congress when Representative John Hostettler from Indiana, accused Democrats of waging a "war on Christianity" on the floor of the House when he blasted them for trying to amend a $409 billion defense spending bill with language condemning the 'coercive and abusive' proselytizing at the school. After 30 minutes of the usual hissing and spitting, a compromise version of the bill was passed: it struck out condemnation of the school but required reports to lawmakers on its religious climate...reports that can be and will be quietly dropped in the wastebasket.

One of the oldest tactics The Lardbutters have used piously and continuously for centuries is the entrapment of children. They know that if they preach loudly and as often as possible to the little ones, the tots are more likely to grow up believing what they heard when they were young. If a kid is scared witless about going to some hell when he's in kindergarten and grade school, he'll still have emotional and psychological remnants of that terror when he's 60.

A case in point hit the national news in 2005 when a Parish School District in Ponchatoula, Louisiana was served a restraining order by a judge who ruled that prayer must be stopped in all school-sponsored events.[2] The argument against the Parish was that the school tried to promote creationism in the classroom, had a preacher coming in and giving out free pizza in the lunchroom while he was lecturing and proselytizing and was forcing the kids to pray to Jesus. The Parish is appealing the ruling to the 5th Circuit Court of Appeals and no doubt will continue to fight 'til their hell freezes over.

It is interesting to note that in America's beginning a number of people who came to its shores did so in the hope of escaping religious intolerance in their home countries. True to religious procedure, many of them then turned right around and displayed the very behavior they had said threatened them. The Salem Witch Trials are a very well known illustration of this. The young girls that were tortured and murdered are now known through laboratory testing to have knowingly or unknowingly been fed mind-altering substances and so were in some sort of manic state. The fire breathing clerics who condemned the lasses wouldn't have cared a whit had they known—it was too much fun telling the community that they were in the arms of The Devil and must be destroyed.

Has our species outgrown such stupidity? Nah. For

proof we can look at the recent death of a 23 year old nun in Romania who was bound to a cross, had a towel stuffed in her mouth and was left in a cold room without food or water for three days.[3] The monk who ordered it, one Daniel Corogeanu, said he was trying to "take the Devil out of her." Will he be prosecuted along with the four nuns who helped him? Maybe. The Romanian Orthodox Church suspended Corogeanu pending an investigation but he refused to obey their ruling, so the Brat mindset that is sure it is right about everything is ready to fight it out. Isn't it interesting that it's always girls or women who are said to be taken by the Devil? The dear old Patriarchy wouldn't want to blame one of its own, now would it? It shouldn't be a surprise that as of 2005 there still was an authorized class on exorcism offered at The Vatican.

As a species we are stuffed shirt proud of our *modern* technology and advancements yet we use and are used by archaic religious teachings to further all of the bilious traits of childishness. That the ability to control others is at the top of the list is obvious and we see the current need to be right becoming a more and more popular tool to consolidate and strengthen that need for power. Those who act as the voices of the various religions and the different splinters within them have no qualms about exaggerating or lying to 'prove' they are right—all the time and in every way. While trumpeting that they speak for a god, they have become as adept as The Quackers in the use of sound bites and our old friend spin and every utterance is used to prove that what is being said is the one way, the only right way of thinking. At the same time, factions that normally would be rivals for membership and money have no trouble bleating the same slogans if there is a larger commitment to the religion as a whole.

This tactic was so popular during the 2004 Presidential elections that it was 'blessed' by the top levels of such seemingly diverse Christian groups as the Catholic and the Baptist—both could hook their oil tankers to such phrases as *family values*. No one was supposed to question what kind of family or whose values were being talked about. If someone did, and there were a few who had the guts to ask, they were immediately drowned out by a sanctimonious chorus that labeled them as not just un-godly, but evil. Worse, the even more valid query about the disappearing separation of church and state was denounced by them as un-American. If the Lardbutters could make sure they could put their own kind in charge of the political landscape, then their own power would increase by quantum leaps. Yes, they did and yes, it has. Christianity took center stage in the good old U.S. of A. and in the ways of Brat greed is still vying for more control. Such a development is bad enough for the country in question; it is disastrous on a planetary scale.

While we're busy slapping ourselves on the back for all of our great modern advancements it would be wise to stop and realize that in areas that really matter to the future of the species and our planet, we have not moved a step out of the brain locked position we were in a millennium ago. As stated before, we are now, this minute, engaged in Religious Wars that are no different in their rationales than they were before we had invented indoor plumbing.

As if the wars were not enough childishness on an organizational level Brat behavior has the Catholic Church reeling from the scandal caused by its cover up of pedophile priests.[4] The identification of abuse was not confined to just a few church fathers or even just a few parishes; it was rampant in the whole of the Catholic Church in America. By the spring of '02 more than 2000 priests had been specifically identified and accused and as the number of cases grew it became painfully clear that for years the hierarchy simply sent the guilty child molesters to a different parish where they could start all over again. Why? Back to childishness…if they admitted to any wrongs then they couldn't keep saying they were right about everything. If they couldn't say they were right about everything they could lose control and if they lost control they would lose power and, of course, money. If a religion claims to be the one and only that is right, it can't take a chance of being told it is wrong.

As the numbers increased and the blame spread from dioceses in Boston to Los Angeles, from St. Louis to Bridgeport, from Cincinnati to Dallas and Palm Beach, the top autocrats made sure that the only ones who would take a fall would be lowly in rank. There were numerous Bishops and Cardinals who knew from the beginning what was going on. Were they publicly chastised? Barely. Some were actually promoted and re-stationed to Rome and The Vatican. Yes, the Church did lose candidates for the priesthood and had to pay millions of dollars in retribution but from a bankroll in the billions, it was just spare change. The word from the top was to fight it all the way and only pay when absolutely necessary and then just ride it out. Sure enough, the squabble was still going strong at the end of 2005.

Christianity is not the only religion that operates from the dogma of power and control. Islam uses it with the same strong-arm tactics and aims as the people of Afghanistan learned under the rule of the Taliban when its fanatic militia took over the country. Under the guise of its War On Terrorism, the U.S. invaded the country and did, for a short moment, bring the Taliban down. Did it go quietly into the night? Of course not. In mid September the country held a general election. Only 50% of the population voted because a lot of people didn't trust those already in power and were afraid of retribution by the Taliban. American troops were still fighting and dying there and were going to be staying for a long time. The Mullahs, the religious leaders of the sect, vowed to stay the course and loudly encouraged rebellion in the name of Allah. They also made sure they got most of the millions of dollars of value from the poppy growers who were afraid to deny them. Cocaine is a bad drug but it can easily finance a long lasting war and if the battle is being fought for the good of a god, who cares.

Self-righteousness is just another term for egotism but it is the granite corner stone of all religions. With it the leaders of all of them can meddle in people's lives to the point of absurdity. One of most widely used incursions is the insistence that approval for the practice of Patriarchy comes directly from a god. Since the three major systems were first invented, the idea that the one god of each was a Father figure, from the Latin *pater*, and that *man* was created in his image has prevailed. Women were said to be an after thought and were really only created for man's benefit. From the beginning the female had no status, no rights and no say-so in her own life. Some progress has been made in recent years in some countries, but most women in this, our *modern* world are little or no better off than they were 10 centuries ago. They are still kept in slavery, used for sex and procreation, are unpaid workers, and are looked down on by a large number of the male population.

In some parts of the world girl babies are still killed simply because they are girls. In most of the Arab countries women still cannot go out of the house alone or uncovered from head to toe, cannot be educated, are married off by their fathers to men they may not even know and they cannot own property. Since these regulations are defended as coming straight from the mouth of Allah, there is little hope the ladies can look forward to any change. Moreover, in Iraq some of the women serving in a legal capacity to write a plan for the Constitution were assassinated to send a message to others to keep quiet.

In some arenas where women have at least had some opportunity to fight for more freedoms, the opposition of the patriarchal religious 'fathers' is seen to be growing. The fight about birth control and abortion in the U.S. gained strength for those against the female's legal right to make decisions about her own body functions and liabilities both before and after the Presidential race of 2004. Using the old claptrap about *family values* again and again, the conservative right wing predicted that the country would be throwing itself into the pits of hell if the un-godly liberals got back any power. To hear it told there would be a huge rise in the number of abortions that would cause the death of 'babies', there would be a heinous wave of people having out of marriage sex and female promiscuity would take over the country. In the basic religious propaganda there was the implied message that all of the potential problems could be blamed on women who weren't smart enough to make good decisions. On top of all that there were snide warnings about the gays and lesbians—men and women who didn't know their place in the world and would be a danger to all.

Never was there one whiff of debate about those women who may not be cut out to be mothers, about those who have trouble getting along with children, about those whose physical health might be threatened by pregnancy and childbirth or about those whose mental, emotional and intellectual skills would be more valuable to themselves and society in other ways—ways that might include science, art, education, medicine or—a god forbid—politics. The Lardbutters knew that their childish insistence on keeping women *in their proper place* would sell when promoted as being dictated by a Supreme Being.

It follows that one of the greatest disservices done to the billions of women on the planet is the idea promoted by religion that women are indeed not smart enough to make their own choices and must be told what to do, when to do it and how to do it. Advertised as a god's way of *taking care* of what is labeled the lesser sex, it gives man final authority in all areas of life from the least important to the most crucial. It is this religious teaching that kept women from any real education for so long and which is still depriving them of it in major arenas of world activity. While there is some hope that the technological ages will even the educational playing field to some degree, it must be remembered that technology alone does not help women advance in an environment controlled by men.

Yes, Boys...we know there are a lot of you out there who do not fit the patriarchal mold and that you use your intelligence and skill to try and change the dreary landscape. We also know that you are not in very good positions of power and we hope you work to change that—for yourselves and for the world. Thank you.

One of the strongest icons that The Lardbutters use to frighten people into believing what they want them to is a classic—The Devil or Satan. Patterned more or less on Hades, the Greek God of the Underworld, this figure even looks like something invented thousands of years ago. Adorned with horns and a tail this caricature of supposedly ultimate evil comes right out of the monster stories kids are told to make them behave and, of course, it is used in the same way by the churches today.

Keep in mind that originally The Devil was said to be a blessed angel who sat next to the God. What happened?...just the usual as far as the oily teachings go...he disagreed with that God. Hmmm...Seems there's another prime example of Brat behavior here: one side can't stand having its supremacy being questioned; the other can't stand being out of the power loop. From the beginning of humanity's story telling about the actions of the gods of the Over and Under worlds, the said beings have been at each other's throats. Suffice it to say, there could be no greater example of the gods imitating man's childishness then that seen in their continuous battles for power.

Fear is the most widely used religious tool. Congregations are battered with warnings of Hell almost every time they sit in the pews. Most of them take pride and some comfort in thinking they are among The Chosen and hope that they will be spared. They also hope that it's still OK for them to lie, cheat and steal like those preaching to them as long as they keep telling their god that they are sorry. Sometimes even that isn't necessary—today a practicing Catholic can literally believe and say out loud that greed is good even though it is supposedly one of the church's Seven Deadly Sins. Anyway, all any good Catholic has to do is take a quick peek at the Vatican where greed and amassing money are a way of life—quite a giggle that would make the imaginary Satan proud.

When The Lardbutters, The Polliwogs and The Money Bunnies march in step to the same drumbeat of childishness, humanity teeters on the edge of chaos and doesn't even see it. Until we, as a species, grow up enough to question ideas that are said to be right simply because someone says so, we haven't much of a chance of dealing with ourselves and our environment in a mature fashion. Fortunately there are a few adults working diligently to expand our understanding of what is real and what is not. For those who want to start an exciting new journey, Quantum Physics holds out some wonderful possibilities.

The on going exploration of the process called The String Theory is one of the most exciting. In it the entire idea of a Universe is turned upside down with the potential for Alternate Realities—including ours—that are made up of teeny tiny *strings* of energy that change and adapt to fit the circumstances and requirements of whatever it is they are currently creating. These little blips of conscious energy are so small we will probably never be able to see them but it is now pretty certain they exist.

No doubt the religions will continue to try to pretend that science either doesn't exist or is wrong but, hopefully, new ideas will at the very least awaken a few people.

With that there is a slim chance of growing up...a little.

CHAPTER 5

The Pill Piddlers

Health and Medicine

Suffice it to say that there are many, many doctors, nurses, interns, aides and medical scientists who are honest, who are good at their jobs, who really care for the sick and dying and who deserve better than average paychecks and respect. At the same time there are also many who are only in the health and medicine community for their own or their company's financial and market place advantage. These **Pill Piddlers** live by the same childish traits of greed and egotism as their counterparts in the political, corporate, communication and religious arenas and because of that they actually are known to put people in jeopardy rather than helping them out of it.

Most notorious are the pharmaceutical companies that adhere to the Money Bunnie rules concerning the sanctity of money but use the Quackers methods to acquire it even when their products are dangerous or useless. An hour or two spent monitoring TV quickly illustrates the suffocating number of expensive commercials aired in the attempt to lure buyers to medicine that may or may not be of any real worth to them and which may actually cause them harm. In America the number of people who live in constant and disruptive fear of some disease or illness that they have never had and are unlikely to have in the future is truly staggering. These poorly informed consumers are so worried about an ailment they heard about through the ads that many of them have become addicted to medicines they didn't need in the first place.

Like everything else in our current society certain drugs rise and fall in calculated and well-financed trends of popularity. When a *new* medicine is ready to be launched on the marketing pad, the corporation behind its manufacture produces an ad campaign that saturates all forms of The Media. In many cases the amount spent to promote it equals or exceeds the cost of its discovery or invention. The company may publicly moan and groan about how it is simply trying to recover some of its investment but from the beginning the product was intended to put dollars in the pockets of its stockholders and executives.

One little example from back in the late 90s shows the extent to which companies will go to keep a portion of the market all for itself.[1] On February 2, 1998 Zenith Goldline Pharmaceuticals and Abbot Laboratories put up their dukes in patent court. For three years the companies had been fussing about whether Zenith could market a generic version of *Hytrin,* Abbot's lucrative $500 million a year drug for high blood pressure and prostrate enlargement.

"Abbot makes a million dollars for every day it keeps us off the market," Bill Mentlik, Zenith's lawyer argued in court. "Without a cheaper generic," he warned, "the public is losing."

That 'caring' argument was really just a public statement playing footsie for a more corporate focus. When the courtroom yapping ended for the day, the two sides retreated to the classy Hay-Adams Hotel in Washington, D.C. for a closed-door luncheon where Zenith's lawyers laid out a proposal as a possible end to the legal battle. They offered to become partners in an introduction of the generic drug. Abbot's lawyer declined saying that his company would rather have a straight numbers deal.

No problem—the deal was signed March 31, 1998. Abbot would pay Zenith as much a $2 million a month not to produce its generic—up to a maximum of $42 million. And to show it could play patty cake with everybody Abbot also agreed to pay another rival, Geneva Pharmaceuticals, even more—a tidy $4.5 million a month and as much as $101 million over the life of the contract.

Oddly, for once the backroom conniving didn't work the way they planned when an antitrust investigation denied their deal and so Zenith's generic was able to hit the market in late 1999. What was not and is not talked about is the fact that the price of a generic medicine like

Hytrin and all of its non-generic equivalents rises immediately when the corporations face any reduction in profits. As the lawyer said, only those taking the medicine lose. During the years of the court fight over *Hytrin*, Abbot's revenues from the drug's sales were calculated at about $2 billion and most of it was pure profit.

While the Zenith/Abbot case caused the most public outcry, many companies have been involved in similar battles.[2] The drug *Tamoxifin*, a breast cancer drug, *Cardizem* CD, a heart medication and *K-Dur*, potassium supplement and *Cipro*, an antibiotic have all fought the availability of generic copies. One of the most ironic developments in the wars between generic and non-generic drugs concerned Merck & Co. and its non-generic pain relief pill called *Vioxx*. In 2000 clinical researchers raised doubts abut it when they indicated its used might increase the risk of heart attack. A publicized study in March of that year found that patients taking *Vioxx* were five times more likely to have heart attacks than those taking *Naproxen*, the generic counterpart. At the time Merck was quoted as saying that there was no defect in *Vioxx* and that it was simply that the generic had cardio-protective qualities that its product did not. Still, it had to pull Vioxx off the market in September of '04 and by '05 Merck was fighting a hefty number of lawsuits brought in connection to the hundreds of wrongful death and injury cases caused by its drug.

Just like the Brat who wants all the toys, the medical corporations willingly pay huge lawyers fees and court costs to defend their monopolies and will continue to do so as long as they can since those payments are far, far less than the profits made from the 'one-of-a-kind' medications. Today almost any prescription medicine that takes $65.00 out of the buyer's pocket returns an average $60.00 pure profit to the manufacturer.

As almost everyone with a TV knows, one of the most heavily advertised drugs on the market at the beginning of the 21st Century was the male sexual enhancer *Viagra*. Syrupy ads crowded the airwaves at all hours of the day and night in order to make men believe how easily they could again have the same kind of sex drive they had as teenagers. Couched in romantic, if always seemingly married scenarios that showed the 'little woman' excited about the potential 'loving' encounters, the real message was aimed solely at the male libido. Female arousal was not the concern but it was implied she should be happy with her man's increased virility.

One could say then that it was a real kick in the balls for the manufacturer when it came out in mid 2005 that nearly 100 men had gone blind after taking *Viagra*. As always there was a rush of ads proclaiming that the potential for loss of sight was 'minimal' and that the advantages far out weighed the possibility of blindness. Yeah, tell that to the men who have to grope for the rest of their lives to even *find* their women.

In discussing medical disaster there is a word that everyone should make sure is added to a working vocabulary—the word *iatrogenic*. It means medicine or surgical procedures that are specifically dangerous to the patients involved.

Under its heading come the 2.2 million people who suffered adverse reactions to drugs given to them by doctors and the 7.3 million people who had unnecessary or totally wrong surgical procedures performed on them plus the 8.9 million who were wrongfully hospitalized. The total number of iatrogenic deaths in 2003 was said to be 783,936 but it was also said that only 20% of iatrogenic acts were even reported which would make a real number for that year about 15,678,720 million. It's hard to fathom what the numbers would be today as they have definitely gone up dramatically. Why?

Because for over 8 decades organized medical groups and the pharmaceutical companies have been using lawyers, bribes, lobbyists, insurance companies and the strong arm of the Food and Drug Administration to corrupt officials so that they pass laws that remove the possibility of competition. In an unusually candid public remark, Dr. Herbert Ley, a former FDA Commissioner said: "the thing that bugs me is that the people think the FDA is protecting them. It isn't. What the FDA is doing and what the public thinks it is doing are as different as night and day."

For those who would like more information there are a number of detailed web sites for iatrogenic medicine on the Internet. Check them out.

Anyone who pays even a small bit of attention to news knows there is a major political fight going on over the future of medical coverage for Americans. He or she also knows that since taking office the Bush Administration's goal has been to reduce, cripple and, when possible, destroy completely the program known as Medicare. Touting what he called a 'political mandate' after re-election in '04, George W. began going around the country—at taxpayers' expense—to sell his ideas on what he called *Privatization*. This slippery plan would make people responsible for their own health coverage through investment accounts that might or might not give them any benefits at all. What it actually would do is leave the healthcare pricing and benefits up to the private insurance companies where there would be no assurance of quality and no guarantee of minimum coverage. In other words, it would be the HMOs deciding who would get what and for how much—the same HMOs that for years have been reducing drug coverage at the same time they were canceling all, repeat *all*, coverage for millions of citizens.

Charging forward with proposals to make the changes, the 109th Congress, all of whom have complete and paid for government coverage as U.S. Reps, seem determined to repeat the Republican objections that were heard when Medicare was brought into being 36 years ago. After all, they don't think it's right to use the citizen's tax money to take care of said citizens—that money needs to be available for projects that reward those who contributed to the elections of those now in the House, Senate and White House. It needs to go as serious pay back to those who control the insurance companies, the pharmaceuticals and the company owned hospitals and clinics. Pork may be called the other white meat but it is decidedly the healthy alternative for the Pill Piddlers who wallow in the mud with the politicians.

One of the most lucrative wallows is found in what are labeled Beauty products. Billions of dollars are spent annually by people who have been convinced that 'looks' are the most important of all human attributes.

One such batch of goodies to hit the airwaves with a resounding blare was for dental products called 'whiteners' The little gems ranged from icky strips like band aids that people were supposed to sleep with on their teeth to liquids and pastes that needed to be used continually for a specific period of time. The come on was that the person's smile would not be attractive unless the teeth were completely, totally and forever a glistening white. From the fact that the ads continue to run month after month and year after year it seems the spiel is working. That doesn't really mean that the merchandise is particularly good or that whether people use it or not is of value—what it means is that the companies involved are raking in the dough and will continue to try to out advertise and out sell all competition.

As always, the message is that if you're not pretty or handsome, you don't count and the criteria for what is *pretty* changes at the whim of corporate say so. If the companies decided that pink teeth for girls and blue teeth for boys were economically viable the advertising for the corresponding beauty products would swamp the Media. Now, however, white teeth are good but white hair is not, which means there are probably more senior citizens with dyed hair today than were even alive 50 years ago.

While it is undeniably true that medical science has made huge advancements in the past and many diseases that used to kill or disable thousands are not now a threat in the rich countries. Such everyday maladies as measles, whooping cough and mumps that used to destroy generation after generation of children have become so rare in the U.S. that they are seldom even mentioned. Everything from dentistry to optometry has been brought happily into our present. The average American life expectancy has jumped from the 40s just a century ago to the 70s today and many of those elders lead normal everyday lives.

Two things raise flags of potential concern, however.

First, there is the growing awareness that the germs that created a lot of the sickness in the past have been or are mutating and no longer respond to the antidotes that previously kill them off. Antibiotics are becoming more of a threat than a cure as they are over prescribed and over used. Doctors still get them as free samples and many continue to hand them out like lollipops.

Secondly, the statistics that apply to the richer countries are not true for what is called The Third World. In Africa particularly, the death toll from such paltry things as the measles is staggering and there is the on-going horror of continental starvation, HIV deaths and a vast number of serious illnesses caused by having to drink heavily polluted water. How heavily polluted? It's like having to drink out of the sewer. Try that on a three year old or your grandmother and see how long they survive!

Every once in a while there is a blip on the international scene that sends politicians into sanctimonious lectures about how the people on the 'dark' continent need to be helped—the yapping lasts a few days, bits of money and aid are promised and then the whole issue fades from sight. After all, those people can't buy our products, vote for us or help us control the world. The Brats prescription says: Don't take an aspirin and don't call us in the morning.

According to the World Health Organization, more than 11 million people a year were killed in 2005 by the top five diseases in the developing world. Respiratory ailments, HIV, diarrhea, malaria and tuberculosis were the five named but it is known that many millions more die from dozens of other kinds of illnesses and the numbers will continue to grow.

Like it does in other areas of our existence the *technology* of health care wields a double-edged sword. It holds promise of great advancements and cures and it threatens with enormous dangers. As long as the pharmaceutical and insurance companies are in charge it is an even bet that the money from advancement in process and procedure will be the driving force behind them all. Pills and medications will hit the market to make money, surgical devices will be promoted to make money and hospitals will continue to raise the cost of treatment in order to make more money.

Today it would be too much to ask that The Pill Piddlers suddenly grow up and start to act like thinking, caring adults. They are so much a part of the concentration of childishness that is running the world that to expect them to mature would be useless. That they are directly involved with the health and well being of millions is a given, that those at the top of their organizations truly don't give a hoot is one of the saddest conditions imaginable. Yes, we know that there are many good doctors, nurses, etc. but they don't run the show and so people die while The Piddlers piddle away lives and good health for money. If that idea gives you a case of heartburn, don't worry you can always get hooked on *Nexium*. You are sure to have heard of it—the manufacturer spends $663,000 a day on its advertising.[3]

CHAPTER 6

The Gutterswipes

Modern Culture

Originally the word *culture* was directly linked to *agriculture* and had no other meaning whatsoever. Since farming was the basis for as well as the main activity in most early settlements around the globe, it's not too surprising that over time the definition gradually widened as people created and practiced other means of livelihood. The word grew to signify all the elements of a particular brand of social activity. For example, to those who have some knowledge of ancient history, the statement Greek Culture can bring to mind images of the Acropolis, wine filled amphorae and stylish paintings of the gods, goddesses and storybook heroes. To those who actually don't care much about the past it might serve as a brief recollection of the 2004 Olympics. Both reflect a *symbolic* snapshot of a cultural development.

In the olden days, different types of people valued different things so that 'cultures' grew in a vast variety of ways. Some were based on valor and what today would be called military might. Some were locked into the whim of their leaders who might or might not care about the welfare of the population. All, in one form or another, claimed to be acting in accordance with whatever gods or spirit beings were said to be talking to them. When ancient societies are examined from a historical point of view they generally are lumped into brackets that proclaim them as being good or bad—often there is little room for any perspective as to why a culture might have gone down one path and not another.

A striking example is the monster Attila the Hun. His name evokes an instant reaction of horror and disgust supported by the stories of massacre and murder, he and his troops inflicted on those they conquered. Little if anything is said about how those troops were forced to act as they did. Attila was one of the early egomaniacs who took great pride in being feared so his own men knew that if they ever dared to question him or his actions they would be killed on the spot. The *culture* we remember would make Attila happy since it is his ego that still reigns over his place in history. The fact that the Mongolian Steppe from which the Huns came had undergone a terrible shift in weather that made it uninhabitable just then is hardly, if ever, mentioned.

Today the whole idea of culture has become so commercialized that it really only means what sells and where. The concept itself is now based on advertising demographics that split potential buyers into groups defined by gender, age and what part of a country they come from. Those in charge of such flimflam can be known as **The Gutterswipes** because they do work really hard to make people swallow the gook that they scrape from the bottom of the barrel—no matter how unpalatable or foolish. Their childish arrogance can be seen in all forms of society's fluctuations and, as always, would be laughable if not so damnably stupid.

One of the arenas where it is most noticeable is in what's called *style*—the kind of clothing, accessories, jewelry, and beauty products that are pushed because they are the moments *in* choices. The catch to this is that the *style* being pushed at any given time will only be allowed to stay popular for a very short sales period. Anyone watching the hemlines of women's skirts over the last 75 years can in any fall predict to an inch as to where they will be for the next spring—the winter length was set in the previous summer. The exact science of such a useless appraisal is always based on how quickly a change must be made in order to get women to feel out of style or even dowdy or ugly so that the latest new merchandise will fly off the shelves.

What's amazing about the whole process is that the clothes do not need to be pretty, becoming or even barely practical—all that matters is getting them sold. It has been said from time to time that some designers actually detest women and must take great pride in making them look awful or enormously silly. Whether true or not, it does speak to some of the ridiculous clothes that have been foisted on the public over the years—clothes that were bought and worn in public for all to see. The

Gutterswipes could care less if what they promote is unbecoming, as always it's the bottom line that counts—the one scrutinized by the financial department, not the one on the bottom of a skirt.

In the style market the age of the buyer is catered to with all the sincerity of the Brat lying to get what it wants. Since it has been *proved* (by advertising Quackers) that teenage girls and young women are the most easily convinced to buy whatever is said to be hot, they have become the most cherished of targets. On and off for several seasons they were told that the navel and stomach along with the top of the hips should be bare, that it was un-cool to cover the flesh in those areas and that to be in style they must conform. Never mind that the 'look' was both tacky and stupid, it was what all their idols were paid to say they preferred so it was to be considered perfectly wonderful. To ram home the message, those same idols…singers and TV and movie stars…were paid big bucks to show up in ads, on the street and on stages and sets wearing the low cut pants and skirts and short-cropped tops. The jewelry biz got in on the parade with studs and rings for the pierced navel. Did it all sell? As our grandparents would say, "indubitably!" Half naked kids slouched down the street of towns all over America totally convinced that they were at the shining top of the cultural heap.

Naturally the boy-Os couldn't be left out of such a rad scam. At the same time the girls went bare belly up teenage boys were told it was not just macho but slick to do the same. Not only were their jeans and pants slung so low the top 4 inches of their boxers could be seen from across the street but the material at the bottom of the legs dragged on the ground. Rap singers and their bands were compensated royally for showing off the look. The 'style' finally seemed to have run its course when the merchandise for the fall of '05 was being prepared and it was announced that in the coming spring the bare look would definitely, positively and unconditionally be OUT! What had happened was that the youngsters had bought so much that their closets were full which absolutely made it time to roll out the next hyped trend so the kids couldn't keep wearing that terribly unstylish stuff they had just bought. The Gutterswipes were ready and willing to see to it that the *culture* of clothing would move right along.

For years what passes for culture in America has been what is seen on TV and in the movies plus whatever is stressed by the music industry. As such, the true meaning or interpretation of *art* is no longer any sort of criteria for what the society considers when validating itself. If something, anything, makes money, it is immediately pushed forward as a major benchmark so its success can be copied and this brings us once again to...sports.

It is difficult today to try and visualize an overall impression of a country without its favorite games. Many countries use the word National so that a society's pride can be tapped publicly. In the U.S. the leagues for a lot of major sports use both National and American in order to square off in blow out matches at the end of a game's season. The impact on the culture that such events unveil is truly amazing and weird and often shows a tidy supply of childish traits in the process.

Owners tossing around millions of dollars in salaries and athletes demanding those millions for playing a game highlight our old standards of greed, selfishness and ego. Arrogance and revenge are showcased when they fight rival teams and managers. Anger and schoolyard fussing is seen in confrontations with each other and with umpires and referees, and even, on occasion, an unsuspecting cameraman. Fear and derision heats up when a team does poorly on the national stage.

Over and over the phrase "winning is everything" is heard by all the participants and then that idea slops over into the culture as a whole. The fear of loss, of not winning, drives whole segments of society, segments of it that may or may not have the faintest clue about what such a one-way belief can mean…People forget that it is literally, as well as statistically, impossible to *win* all the time in every aspect of life. It would mean being PERFECT. Not only is the concept childishly foolish it is exceedingly harmful and we see people trying to live it all the time. In sports the fear of loss is so profound that it led to the steroid crisis. That fear is so deeply ingrained that it's not uncommon for fans to hiss and boo and throw things from the stands when a player or a team is doing poorly. The *culture* feeds on itself like a vampire on the blood and sweat of its idols and icons and cannot stomach it when they don't live up to its impossible expectations.

As noted when discussing the actions of The Polliwogs, the political use of sporting events to further patriotic sentiment rose to an all time high after 9/11. The effort to marry the two cultural opposites took center stage and, years later, in 2005 was still being exploited. While the singing or playing of the National Anthem and America the Beautiful, before or during a break in the game, had been a minor distraction for decades the all out staging of the songs has become standard. What the playing of sports has to do with national security or potential danger is irrelevant, it now leads the pack as one of the most televised avowals of patriotism. That the process was used to raise money for the victims of the hurricanes Katrina and Rita was one of the few times it actually was of benefit...most of the time it's just theater that plays to base emotions and the culture condones it.

The culture also thinks it's just fine that the main sporting events are run by and performed by males. Female athletes not only have no chance in even the imaginary hell of commanding the big wages or TV coverage as the men, they can barely compete. For example, the WMBA, Women's' Basketball Association, runs it championship play offs at the end of the major baseball season so it won't have to compete with the male hoopsters.

An illustration of how childish the male ego can be when challenged on what it thinks of as its own turf was highlighted after the '05 Indianapolis 500...the Indy.[1] At that time the most advertised and talked about feature of the race was the qualifying and excellent driving of one Danica Patrick, a young woman with good skills and good looks. The looks didn't matter in her historic 4th place finish but naturally were a large part of the hype before, during and after the competition even though many sportscasters advised that she was a racer to watch and one who would be a major part of events in the future.

Because her performance was so good and had helped raise viewer percentages to a high not seen in years,

Bernie Ecclestone, the boss of Formula One, the top racing organization in the U.S., called her with congratulations. Not satisfied with a simple "you did a good job," Ecclestone managed to stick his foot in his mouth not just once but twice. First he commented in an interview and then told Danica personally over the phone that "Women should all be dressed in white like all other domestic appliances." Ah yes, Bernie…women should be put back in the kitchen or laundry room.

As expected the airing of his comments did not flood the front pages of the Sports Sections of any major news outlets but were buried in the back where advocates of the male culture hoped they would quickly fade away. They did. After all it's OK if an important guy like Bernie loses his cool once in a while, but the slip up can't be made into a negative bulls-eye on the target of masculine ego.

As we've seen the childish need to be right is the backbone of every culture and has been for millennia. By insisting that it is better than its competition, a country can start a war, starve a population, destroy an environment, isolate a rival, and make fun of any people and customs that get in its way. Sometimes the results are so dumb it takes a huge stretch of imagination to acknowledge they really are happening.

One such occurrence happened shortly after the government of France disagreed with the American invasion of Iraq. A number of U.S. Congressmen were so insulted that one of them stood up in the hallowed halls to demand that the oil cooked potatoes universally called French Fries should be called Freedom Fries. *Freedom Fries?* By the spokesman from a country that had just *invaded* another? Yup. He was kidding, right? Nope. Yes, a lot of people did laugh but a lot more thought it was appropriate. If you can claim that you are always *right* you can get away with huge cauldrons of nonsense and people are afraid to point it out because that might make them seem wrong or, at least, not right.

One of the most pervasive cycles of humanity's cultural history shows the up and down flow of the level of acceptance of real intelligence. Through the ages there have been periods when being smart was considered positive. Each was followed closely by a deliberate shift from those in power who did not want people to understand what they were doing. In each case the culture itself was changed or diluted so that citizens would accept it—keeping the peasant ignorant is standard procedure in Brat Flak.

In the modern world it is so easy to do that The Gutterswipes make use of it 24/7. They are confident enough in the strength of their power that they can slap into place types of control that in sentient times would be thought outrageous. Consider—by the middle of '05 the only non-corporate broadcasting outlet, The Public Broadcasting Service or PBS was attacked on all sides by individuals and coalitions who think that the idea of *tolerance* is dangerous. At the risk of sounding 'liberal' it has to be said that it was the conservative right that put forth a scheme to cut off funding by claiming that PBS showed 'political bias'. Those people whose own bias was not only well documented but proudly and continually stated then put their own partisans at the top of the PBS executive chain and covertly installed Republican consultants in place to monitor—read *snoop*—and call in to a hotline at The White House. Their job was to report on how far Bill Moyer's program NOW was wandering from the approved talking points of the Administration.

According to them the term *public* is to be defined as allowing a voice to half the people all the time and to half the people none of the time. By constantly accusing The Media as being leftist and keeping public awareness at a near zero level they can overturn the whole structure from within.

On June 23rd, 2005 Patricia S. Harrison, former co-chair of the Republican National Committee was selected as the new President of the Corporation For Public Broadcasting, the CPB...talk about political bias. For once the process was criticized when CPB Inspector General Kenneth Konz reported that Kenneth Tomlinson, the former chairman of the CPB broke federal law by interfering with the programming. Specifically the report stated that Tomlinson violated the Public Broadcast Act of 1967.[2] Stations that appeal to intelligence do not fit the Brat's agenda for a worthwhile Media. It wants trivia, twaddle and out of the box emotion.

A perfect example was the constant and blaring coverage of the Michael Jackson trial although the word 'trial' might be a bit out of sync considering it really was a staged vaudeville skit. As usual with such a mammoth flapdoodle, every channel and every network showed the proceedings over and over and over...It was the kind of hot topic that made news desks, producers, advertisers and accountants happy for weeks. Why? They could bury anything and everything else behind it. As one of the most perfect examples of *drivel* seen in years it pushed serious events right out the window and the star performer was, without any doubt, a perfect figurehead for childishness at the top echelon of our *culture*.

One bright little spark in the smog of the planet's cultural bog was the '05 release of the fifth Harry Potter Book—*Harry Potter and the Half Blood Prince*. It and all the previous volumes by J. K. Rowling were well written, ingenious, clever in plot and intellectually stimulating. All over the world the series had convinced millions of children and a sizeable number of their elders that reading was good. They may have to search far and wide to find books that even come close in interest to Rowling's masterpieces but they are now readers and many will be readers all of their lives. A squib in the news that Pope Benedict XVI had said, while still a Cardinal, that the Potter books were dangerous because they identified magic in a positive way did not put a dent in the sales of the fifth book…it broke record first day figures immediately. We might say there was a little bit of positive magic working there.

Today it is almost an oxymoron to say that there is an American culture at all. It fluctuates so rapidly on the whims of the Money Bunnies, The Pollywogs and The Quackers that the Gutterswipes have to pursue a constant search for more barrels to scrape. What's OK today definitely will be wrong tomorrow; what was a focus for attention yesterday went out the window at midnight. Until individuals grow up enough to understand that their decisions, both large and small, must be made through careful and adult analysis, there is not much hope for a society based on something besides commercialism and hoopla.

We must pity the poor twit who keeps going 'round the same track because he can't read the signs that would show him a new direction — true, the scenes on either side of the road change from time to time but since they're just pictures that are put up to amuse and confuse him he doesn't even know his world is not real.

Living in the *culture* of the childish is like performing in a TV sitcom, the only difference is you don't get to go outside and see what's truly going on between takes.

What must be understood today is that the so-called cultures of the world do not arise naturally from the efforts, activities and choices of national populations. They are spoon fed from the top down and allow no room for deviation from the wishes of those in control. In a somewhat subtler but equal form than the one portrayed in the book 1984, people of the U.S.A. are living under the same type of coercion and mandated behavior that Orwell wrote about. The words *freedom* and *democracy* are plastered on everything from the court system to the schools, from the commercialism of communication to the huge deficiencies in health care, from the strangle hold that the corporations have on their wealth and on the poverty of those beneath them, from the on-going policies of racism and discrimination and, of course, to politics. The labels sound marvelous and have no meaning. Freedoms are systematically being taken away and the democratic process is bought and sold — and stolen.

If the human species somehow is still in existence 100 or 200 years in the future it will mean that at some point the peasants got sick of being bullied and were able to consolidate enough strength to overturn the Brats and their minions. It won't be easy and a lot of innocent people will suffer in the process—still for the welfare of our great, great, great, great.... grandchildren, all other types of living things and the planet itself, it will probably be necessary. It's a given the kiddies will not relinquish their self-proclaimed mandate peacefully since the childish never, ever admit to making a mistake.

At the moment it is difficult to even imagine a culture based on mature choices and adult self-responsibility. It has been such a long time since the world showed even a thin frosting of such attributes that few people alive have any memory of what it felt like. For the sake of the future it can only be hoped that a drastic change for the better will occur in all of the varied type of cultures...if not the years ahead will be a slippery slope indeed.

CHAPTER 7

Finis

Every single day examples and illustrations of humanity's childishness are played out from one end of the globe to the other. If they were all recorded here, there would be no end to the number of pages needed to document them, no time line in sight to finish and no let up in the events that so graphically show how heavily the species is warped by the actions and decisions of the Brats.

The saddest part of all is how billions of people can be kept ignorant of the danger posed by the planetary control exercised by those who refuse to grow up. The millions of sane adults who try valiantly to bring some kind of clarity and a little sanity to the situation are made voiceless and powerless through the deliberate efforts of the kiddies who are running things. It doesn't matter a whit which so-called culture or environment they live in, they are effectively silenced by each and every group that has a part in the current processes that run each and every level of life. The Corporate, The Political and Military, The Communication, The Religious and the Health and Medical are so closely intertwined that nothing slips through the cracks. Trying to get the message out is like trying to teach Sign Language with an audiotape.

Lying, cheating and stealing are so much a way of life that they are enthusiastically copied. The greed that is bolstered by ego shapes the way commerce is constructed and conducted. Violence, cruelty, anger and revenge run the critical parts of the societies of nations, communities and individuals. Stupidity is at the helm of the US Ship of State and is steering its and the world's six billion voyagers straight into the shoals of unnecessary destruction. The lust for power and control grows daily as it creates unworkable situations in every area of existence—it wrecks the environment and refuses to acknowledge it, it allows the massacre of thousands while making plans that will kill thousands if not millions more, it deprives the majority of living beings of the basics for a decent life and then pats itself on the back because it was all so simple to do.

Actually, each and every collection of Brats that is running the world still wants more power, more control, and more money. Each is convinced that it alone is completely and totally right...about everything! While it may not be trumpeted publicly, each believes deeply that it is entitled to and deserves not just to run its piece of the world but everyone else's pieces...the whole bloody pancake. Historically, those who strived for world domination in earlier times eventually were stopped because a group of dissenters rose up to challenge them. Sometimes the reasons for doing so were heroic and gallant, other times it was simply at the urging of an alternate control freak.

If it's hard to picture how bad things are, try imagining a food fight in a school cafeteria where the youngsters are throwing trays and chairs and overturning tables and steam racks. At the same time the bullies in the playground are storming around destroying the swings and slides and beating up on everyone in sight. Kids in the halls are running up and down screaming and stealing from and smashing the lockers. They flood into the classrooms and break desks and blackboards and set fire to the books in the library. A pack of kiddies blows up everything in the science lab while another locks the teachers in a bathroom after getting rid of all the telephones, computers and surveillance cameras in the building. No one on the outside knows what going on and no one cares—it's just cute little children, so what's the problem?

The problem is that the children that are running things aren't cute and the clock is ticking. The schoolhouse of the real world is about to explode. The Brats have taken over and as long as they are allowed to continue their rule there is little hope for the billions they control. It has been said that Growing Up Is Hard To Do and though the lyrics to that song were meant to deal with problems of the teen years it can now be applied to our species as a whole.

OH, GROW UP!

The real pity is that so few people are really aware of the situation. The efforts concocted to keep them ignorant chug along 24 hours a day. The average human is not only deliberately kept uninformed he is also kept over-worked, over-stressed, poorly educated and under-paid. By design he has no time to study the serious questions of existence and little, if any, energy with which to do it. The debt on his credit cards is way over extended, his boss bothers him day and night with extra work, his wife has had to take a job at Wal-Mart, and his mother can't afford her medication and living expenses because his father just lost his pension. On top of all that his son got his girl friend pregnant because no one told him about condoms and then died in combat oversees.

In poor countries it's even worse. There's no work available and no adequate shelter, vandals or militants steal and kill, hundreds die every day from disease and starvation and the population is illiterate.

None of that matters to the Brat Brigade who will happily continue to use all of their now swollen childish talents to get what they want. If lying and coercion aren't working well enough, they haul out the old fear factor with its handy attributes of intimidation and suppression and if they're caught in their lies, they try to pack the courts with buddies who will rule in their favor. They use their ill-gotten power to control every aspect of a society and constantly play political and corporate games to get more. Their arrogance screams loudly about their belief that they are one hundred percent right on everything from war and money to politics and religion. They admit to no mistakes and squelch any criticism of their decisions and choices. They use discrimination and hate to further their aims and encourage the peasants to be suspicious of each other. They babble about freedom ad nauseum while deliberately making sure that the population's rights are removed one by one and en masse. They despise 'the poor' and hope to make them even poorer.

By allowing ourselves to be dominated by the childish, we have also let ourselves become stupefyingly ignorant in all areas of life that matter and there is no end in sight. There is absolutely no question that growing up gets harder and harder to do the longer we let the Brats stay in charge. About all that can be said to the rest of us is Good Luck—we're going to need it—otherwise it really can be…

Finis!

Appendix

Chapter 2

1 "The Best Democracy Money Can Buy" by Greg Palast

2 Jane Spenser, The Wall Street Journal, August 4, 2002

3 Joyce Gannon, The PittsburghPost-Gazette, July 24, 2005 & Ellen Goodman, The Boston Globe, July 24, 2005

4 Sandy Cohen, The Associated Press, November 4, 2005

5 Karren Mills, The Associated Press, July 18, 2000

6 Nedva Pickles, The Associated Press, September 7 & 13, 2000 (Exxon Valdez)

7 William Greider, The Nation, September 19, 2005

Chapter 3

1 The Denver Post, March 10, 2002

2 Alison Mitchell, The New York Times, March 21, 2002

3 Lisa Hoffman, Scripps Howard News Service, May 30, 2002 & Sandra Sobieray, The Associated Press, May 30, 2002

4 Judy Holland, Hearst Newspapers, March 13, 2002

Chapter 4

1 Websters New Collegiate Dictionary, 1950 Edition, page 566

Chapter 5

1 Richard Cohen, The Washington Post, June 12, 2005 & M.E. Sprengelmeyer, The Rocky Mountain News, June 12, 2005 & Dick Foster, The Rocky Mountain News, June 23, 2005 & M.E. Sprengelmeyer and Dick Foster, The Rocky Mountain News, June 23, 2005 & M.E. Sprengelmeyer, The Rocky Mountain News, June 29, 2005

2 Jake Tapper and Clayton Sandell, NBCNews.com, June 9, 2005

3 The Associated Press, June 21, 2005

4 Michael Kelly, The Washington Post, Boston, March 21, 2002 & Ron DePasquale, The Associated Press, Boston, May 7, 2002 & Jim Yardley, The New York Times, August 24, 2002

Chapter 6

1 Sheryl Gay Stolberg, Jeff Gerth, The New York Times, July 23, 2000

2 Andrew Pollack, The New York Times, June 14, 2005

3 The Rocky Mountain News, August 30, 2005

Chapter 7

1 Motor Sports Column, no by line, June 23, 2005

2 Jennifer C. Kerr, Associated Press, November 16, 2005

Printed in the United States
91306LV00012B/21/A